DISCUSSION PAPER 55

THE AFRICA POLICIES OF NORDIC COUNTRIES AND THE EROSION OF THE NORDIC AID MODEL
A comparative study

BERTIL ODÉN

NORDISKA AFRIKAINSTITUTET, UPPSALA 2011

Indexing terms:
Foreign aid
Development aid
Foreign policy
Foreign relations
International cooperation
Aid policy
Denmark
Finland
Norway
Sweden

The opinions expressed in this volume are those of the author and do not necessarily reflect the views of Nordiska Afrikainstitutet.

Language checking: Peter Colenbrander
ISSN 1104-8417
ISBN 978-91-7106-691-6
© The author and Nordiska Afrikainstitutet 2011
Production: Byrå4
Print on demand, Lightning Source UK Ltd.

Contents

Foreword 5

Acronyms and Abbreviations 6

Executive Summary 7

1. Introduction 11
2. Nordic Cooperation and the "Nordic Model" in Development Cooperation 16
3. The Aim of the Policy/Strategy Documents and their Overall Design 22
4. Issue Areas Compared 30
5. Special Features of the Africa Policies of Individual Nordic Countries 42
6. Summary and Conclusions 48

References 53

Table Annex 56

Foreword

This Discussion Paper presents the findings of a comparative study of the "Africa Policies" of four Nordic countries, namely Finland, Sweden, Norway and Denmark. The study was initiated against the backdrop of 1) intense international debate on the future of development aid in general; 2) the realisation that the old aid system dominated by the OECD countries is giving way in significance to aid from emerging powers exclusively designed to promote business relations; and 3) the prominent role private foundations now assume in the aid business relative to the resources allocated towards aid by traditional donors.

This commissioned study, undertaken by NAI Associate Bertil Odén, is designed to test the accepted wisdom that the Nordic countries pursue similar development policies in relation to the Africa continent, both in form and content. The study therefore attempts to identify the areas of "convergence" and of "divergence" in Nordic policies towards Africa through a closer examination of key African policy documents issued by the four countries over the past five years. In the case of Denmark, the Africa Policy was later supplemented by a report of the Danish Africa Commission. In addition to the desk review of the key policy documents, Bertil Odén followed up by conducting interviews with a select group of policymakers and opinion shapers in the four countries. (All the relevant documents can be found on NAI's website.)

To date, little systematic analysis has been undertaken to ascertain the "Nordic character" of the respective countries' development cooperation strategies with the African continent. The study examines current practices in the context of the historical experience of Nordic development cooperation with Africa. As such, this is a first attempt to decode the myth of a common "Nordic development policy," which has undergone major transformations since the 1990s as a result of internal and external factors. Is solidarity with Africa still the *raison d'être* of Nordic development strategy? Or has this been replaced by other pressing priorities, such as promoting Nordic business interests in Africa or new security concerns?

In sum, the study provides additional insights into the changing nature of Nordic development policy towards the African continent and identifies emerging patterns. Although the present study needs to be supplemented with a more detailed empirical investigation, the report provides tentative, but startling conclusions. Among the key findings are that the traditional "Nordic model of development cooperation" has eroded, with individual Nordic countries now heading in different directions. Second, with one exception, African stakeholders were marginally consulted when the policy-guiding documents were prepared.

Professor Fantu Cheru
Research Director
The Nordic Africa Institute

Acronyms and Abbreviations

ACP	Africa, Caribbean and Pacific Countries
APRM	African Peer Review Mechanism (NEPAD)
AU	African Union
CSO	Civil Society Organisation
DAC	Development Assistance Committee (OECD)
EC	European Commission
EU	European Union
EPA	Economic Partnership Agreement
FDI	Foreign Direct Investment
GNI	Gross National Income
GPG	Global Public Good
IFI	International Financial Institutions
IMF	International Monetary Fund
MDG	Millennium Development Goal
MONAP	Mozambique-Nordic Agricultural Programme
NEPAD	New Partnership for Africa's Development
ODA	Official Development Assistance
OECD	Organisation for Economic Cooperation and Development
PGD	Policy for Global Development
RENAMO	Mozambique National Resistance
SADC	Southern Africa Development Community
SADCC	Southern Africa Development Coordination Conference
SSA	sub-Saharan Africa
TRIPS	Trade Related Aspects of Intellectual Property Rights (WTO agreement)
UN	United Nations
WTO	World Trade Organisation

Executive Summary

The gloomy Western "aid fatigue" perspective on sub-Saharan Africa has over the last decade been replaced by a more hopeful one. This change of attitude is based on a number of positive changes in African development during this period, including the increased importance of Africa as a provider of raw materials to the rest of the world.

This development has also piqued the interest of actors other than aid bureaucrats, including international corporations and equity funds. The main trigger, however, has been the entry of the big emerging developing countries (China, India, Brazil and others) on to the African scene: they have seen possibilities all over the place, instead of problems.

This international trend has also influenced the Nordic countries. During 2007–10, four of them – Denmark, Norway, Sweden and Finland in that order – launched new Africa policies/strategies to facilitate a new and broader approach in their relations with African countries and organisations.

The main aim of this comparative study is to examine the similarities and differences between the documents guiding the Nordic countries' Africa policies and to glean comparative insights from a content analysis of the official documents.

The study is organised as follows. It starts with an historical overview of Nordic cooperation with Africa and then outlines the main characteristics and overall objectives of the Africa policy documents of the four Nordic countries. The conclusions derived from the comparison of the documents are summarised and the similarities and main differences between the specific profiles of the four countries are outlined. The aim and role of Africa policies/strategies are discussed, as well as the possible value added by Nordic cooperation and the erosion of the "Nordic aid model". Finally, some suggestions regarding the scope for future Nordic cooperation are presented.

Since the beginning of this millennium, Nordic trade, FDI and other commercial relations with Africa have been growing, albeit modestly. Africa is still a marginal commercial partner for the Nordic countries and vice versa. Among the Nordics, Norway shows signs of slightly more dynamic development in this regard.

The overview shows that there are several traditional Nordic aid priorities common across the guiding policy documents discussed in the study. These include democracy, human rights, gender issues, environment, peace and security, regional integration and a strong emphasis on direct poverty reduction in line with the MDGs.

Similarities between the Nordic countries can also be seen in the choice of a number of other thematic areas, but these rather reflect the fact that the Nordics are following current international trends. Examples are efforts to enhance the inclusion of African countries in a globalising world, private sector development as the main driving force for economic growth, support for adjustment to climate change and cooperation in the field of migration.

The three EU members, Denmark, Finland and Sweden, strongly emphasise and support the EC's importance as an international actor, and also regard the commission as an instrument for boosting their own influence.

There are also a number of differences between the Nordic countries, affording them different profiles.

Denmark is the strongest actor in facilitating Africa's inclusion in a globalising world and in promoting commercial and other relations outside development cooperation with Africa. This fits well with the traditional parallel motives for its development cooperation – solidarity and enlightened self-interest. As a consequence, the instruments supporting efforts by the Danish private sector to increase its engagement in Africa are strengthened. The emphasis on African youth and employment is also a strong Danish feature.

Finland in its development cooperation has maintained the focus on increased sustainable development and the MDGs within traditional long-term bilateral relations. The Finnish document on development cooperation with Africa attempts to combine the re-establishment of bilateral and regional cooperation based on sustainable development and MDG-based poverty-reduction, focusing on sectors and branches in which Finland is internationally competitive. Finnish policy is also strongly framed within the Joint EU-Africa Strategy.

The *Africa in Finnish Foreign Policy* document emphasises the principle of coherence between policy segments in order to serve foreign policy goals. In the Finland-Africa context, this involves strong emphasis on support for the AU and African regional organisations and for regional integration, with a special focus on security and peacekeeping.

Norway is the Nordic country most strongly focused on contributing to global public goods, and is the most active in launching international programmes and initiatives related to global issues, while traditional long-term bilateral cooperation has been put on the back-burner. Norway now has the most politicised aid programme among the Nordics. It is also the only Nordic country to stress the importance of reducing capital outflows from Africa and curtailing international tax havens.

Sweden, with its *Policy for Global Development* dating from 2003, can be regarded as a Nordic frontrunner in terms of policy coherence. The importance of this and addressing conflicts of interest among policy areas in a transparent and constructive manner is also increasingly acknowledged by other Nordic countries. Sweden is also upfront in its emphasis on results-based management.

The focus on increased global public goods, together with the emphasis on private sector development, coherence between policy areas and activities that can be measured more easily reinforces the ongoing international trend towards development cooperation in which the influence of partner countries is gradually reduced. This implies that the Nordic countries' previous strong emphasis on partnership and striving to ensure the ownership by the cooperating partner of aid-supported projects and programmes has weakened, with Finland the exception. This is ironic, given the strong support for the Paris Declaration by all the Nordic countries, but is in line with mainstream policy among DAC members.

African governments today have access to resources other than those provided by Western aid agencies, both from emerging markets and from a larger segment of the private sector. This makes possible a new attitude towards Western governments. Increasingly, African governments, some of them large aid recipients, show less interest in dialogue on issues such as governance, human rights and democracy, traditionally high priorities in the Africa development policy of Nordic countries. Significant efforts are needed to analyse the new framework in which the Nordic relations with Africa will be formed in order to identify new measures and instruments to further Nordic countries' future relations with Africa.

Rather than being an intermediate policy document, the main role of the Africa documents has been to codify existing thinking on development and other issue areas at the specific moment the policy was launched. Operationally, the influence of the Africa documents is normally weak. Another apparent aim of the Africa documents is to signal to the international community and/or the domestic political and public arena that the government of the Nordic country concerned is aware of ongoing changes and intends to meet them.

The traditional "Nordic aid model" has eroded in recent years and the current development cooperation policies of the different Nordic countries in Africa and elsewhere seem to be heading in different directions. In this respect, Nordic countries no longer form the core of a like-minded group. Instead they are moving along different trajectories and in the process becoming part of new donor constellations.

Nonetheless, traditionally close Nordic cooperation in development has persisted in two areas – at the operational level in African partner countries and between Nordic capitals in preparing for meetings of international organisations.

Should the political will for joint or coordinated Nordic policy on development cooperation revive, there are a number of relevant considerations. They include stronger influence on the EU's Africa policy through common preparations and action among the Nordic EU members; more joint analytical work, with the Nordic Africa Institute as one possible arena; strengthened Nordic cooperation in support of African capacity-building; restoring Nordic cooperation to enhance African research capacity; and improved cooperation and a more effective division of labour among Nordic countries in local harmonisation processes in partner countries. A more radical option would be for Nordic countries to divide up the long-term cooperating countries in Africa among themselves so that each assumed responsibility for a few countries and vacated the rest. Each Nordic country would then become a major donor in a few countries, provided the volume of their aid would be consistent with current joint Nordic aid levels.

1. Introduction

This is a study of how Nordic governments are trying to adjust to an ever-changing African environment by working out regional policy documents. Simply put, they are using a static instrument to aim at a moving target. This is obviously a great challenge.

From gloom to glee – the perception of Africa

The gloomy Western "aid fatigue" perspective on sub-Saharan Africa[1] has over the last decade given way to a more hopeful one.[2] This change of attitude is based on the economic and political changes in Africa, among them the ending of some of the domestic and regional armed conflicts; the improved macroeconomic balance in many countries; improved governance in some countries; average economic growth above 5 per cent per annum up to the global financial crisis in a significant number of countries with a longstanding development co-operation record; and last but not least, the increased importance of Africa as a provider of energy, minerals, timber and agricultural commodities to the rest of the world.

African development has also generated increased interest among actors other than aid bureaucrats, including international corporations and equity funds. The main trigger, however, has been the entry of the big emerging developing countries (China, India, Brazil and others) on to the African scene: they have seen possibilities all over the place, instead of problems. South-South cooperation is rapidly expanding. This in turn has alerted traditional external powers in North America and Europe to begin to rethink their positions in order to defend their influence on the continent.[3] The notion of "a new scramble for Africa's natural resources" is frequently used in the business press.

The launching of the African Renaissance concept and the founding of NEPAD in the 1990s were two early signs of emerging change on the African scene. Development since then has broadened relations between Africa and the Nordics – themselves small players in the world economy – although to date rather modestly. While growing trade, investment and other commercial links between the Nordics and Africa are still marginal both in an international comparison and as share of the total of the two groupings.

---

1. In this text, Africa normally refers to sub-Saharan Africa.
2. One recent example is Radelet, S. (2010). *Emerging Africa: How 17 Countries Are Leading the Way*. Washington DC: Center for Global Development.
3. The literature on this topic has proliferated in recent years. A few examples are OECD Development Centre (2009). *The rise of China and India: What's in it for Africa?;* OECD. *Perspectives on Global Development, 2010 Shifting Wealth;* Cheru, F. and C. Obi (eds.) (2010). *The Role of China and India in Africa. Challenges, Opportunities and Critical Interventions.* London: Zed Books; and Brautigam, D. (2009). *The Dragon's Gift. The real story of China in Africa.* Oxford: Oxford University Press.

Combined Nordic exports to Africa increased by around 60 per cent between 2005 and 2008, while imports from Africa doubled. The economic crisis reduced these figures slightly in 2009.[4] Africa's share of total foreign trade is, however, still very low for all the Nordic countries: around or below 1 per cent in recent years, with the export share higher than the import share for all countries except Norway (table 1.1.)

Table 1.1. Nordic countries' foreign trade with sub-Saharan Africa 2005–09 as percentage of total trade

Country	2005	2006	2007	2008	2009
Imports					
Denmark	0.5	0.5	0.4	0.5	0.4
Finland	0.5	0.5	0.5	0.7	0.5
Norway	1.1	1.1	1.3	1.6	1.6
Sweden	0.4	0.4	0.4	0.6	0.9
Exports					
Denmark	0.9	1.0	1.0	1.3	1.3
Finland	1.4	1.5	1.6	1.3	1.4
Norway	0.5	0.5	0.7	0.7	0.7
Sweden	1.3	1.2	1.4	1.8	1.9

Source: Central statistical offices of Denmark, Finland, Norway and Sweden.

The flow of direct investments from the Nordic countries to sub-Saharan Africa has increased modestly, and with the exception of Norway in recent years, is still less than 1 per cent of each country's aggregate FDI.

Table 1.2. Nordic countries' FDI in Africa

Country (currency)	2004	2005	2006	2007	2008	2009
Denmark (DAK bn)	5.7	6.0	6.8	6.0	6.2	
Finland (€ mn)	6	8	13	11	18	9
Norway (NOK bn)	4.1	0.2	2.7	1.1	6.5	
Sweden (SEK bn)	−0.2	−4.0	1.1	−0.8	2.7	0.7

Source: Central Statistics Offices of Finland, Norway, Sweden and Central Bank of Denmark.

Table 1.3 Nordic countries' FDI in Africa as percentage of total

Country	2004	2005	2006	2007	2008	2009
Denmark	1.0	0.9	0.9	0.8	0.7	
Finland		0.2	0.3	0.2	0.3	0.4
Norway	1.4	0.1	2.3	1.7	4.4	
Sweden	−1.3	−2.0	0.7*	−0.3	1.5*	0.3*

* inflow when total net flow is negative

---

4. More detailed data on trade can be found in table 10 in the annex.

The tables thus show that Nordic sub-Saharan Africa trade and investment links remain marginal, with the increase in Norway's FDIs being the exception.

During the same period, aid from the Nordic countries to sub-Saharan Africa increased in absolute terms, while its share of their total aid increased slightly up to 2008. However, judging from the annual aid budgets since then, the trend has stagnated or even reversed. As regards bilateral aid, sub-Saharan Africa's share has, however, remained at a high level (See tables 1a-c in the table annex.) While aid-linked issues still dominate Nordic relations with many countries in sub-Saharan Africa, other aspects are gradually increasing in importance.

This recent international trend has also influenced the Nordic countries. At the end of the first decade of this millennium, four of them – Denmark, Finland, Norway and Sweden – launched new Africa policies/strategies to facilitate a new and broader approach in their relations with African countries and organisations.

In all Nordic countries, relations with Africa up to the late 1990s were dominated by development cooperation. With the exception of South Africa and a few commodity exporters, a significant part of the Nordic foreign trade was directly or indirectly generated by aid-related activities. A summary of the individual Nordic countries' historical and modern relations with Africa at the beginning of the new millennium was published by the Nordic Africa Institute in 2002.[5]

The present study is based on the Africa policy documents produced by the governments of Denmark, Sweden, Norway and Finland (in that order) during the years 2007–10. The amount of empirical evidence regarding the possible impact of these documents is thus very limited. To assess to what extent the policies/strategies imply any changes, a longer perspective is needed, as well as references to sources beyond the Africa policy documents. The comparison also highlights historical and present trends in Nordic cooperation, in particular development cooperation, including the rise and fall of what has sometimes been referred to as the "Nordic aid model".

Aim, method and outline of the study

The main aims as formulated in the agreement for this study are:
1. To undertake a scoping exercise, relying mainly on the main texts produced by the four governments over the past couple of years, and establishing what comparative insights emerge from a content analysis of the official documents.

---

5. Wohlgemuth, L. (ed.) (2002). *The Nordic Countries and Africa. Old and New Relations.* Uppsala: The Nordic Africa Institute.

2. To examine current practices in the context of the historical experience of Nordic development cooperation with African countries, including determining whether solidarity with Africa is still the *raison d'être* of Nordic development strategy.
3. To gain additional insights into the changing nature of Nordic development policy towards Africa, including the financing mechanisms and practices of the Nordic countries.
4. To assess how much space African countries are given in their relationship with Nordic governments and reflect on the implications of the diversity of implementation strategies for state capacity in Africa and the state-citizen relationship.

The following questions will be investigated:
1. In which fields do current Africa policy/strategy documents of the Nordic countries reflect common policy and in which fields do policies differ?
2. What is the role of the Africa policies/strategies in policy towards individual African countries and sub-regions, relative to other policy documents? What is the value added of specific Africa policy-guiding documents in respect of policy towards individual countries and regions in Africa?
3. What is the actual impact of Africa policies/strategies when new country-cooperation strategies are developed? What factors outside the guiding documents can be traced from empirical evidence?
4. Has the Nordic dimension changed and, if so, in which direction? Is Nordic cooperation more or less intense than previously with regard to the four countries' relations with Africa? Is it still possible to talk about a "Nordic aid model"?

The study is based on:
1. A comparison of current Africa policy-guiding documents from Denmark, Finland, Norway and Sweden. (Iceland has no document of this kind, and is therefore not included in the study.)
2. Reading complementary policy and operational documents from the four countries relevant to their Africa relations.
3. Interviewing civil servants, researchers and civil society representatives on the impact of Africa policy documents in real life and of other factors on the implementation of the Africa relations, as well as on their experience of cooperation between Nordic countries in some African countries.
4. Perusing comments and analytical texts of relevance for the study.

Section 2 of this paper provides a brief historical overview of Nordic cooperation with Africa and the concept of the "Nordic aid model". Section 3 outlines the main characteristics of the Africa policy documents of the four Nordic countries and how they relate to other policy documents with an impact on African policy. Section 4 contains conclusions from a comparison of the four countries in a number of focus areas and priority cooperation sectors. In section 5, similarities and the specific profiles of the four countries are summarised. Finally, in section 6 conclusions are provided, including reflections on the current role and possible value added of Africa policy-guiding documents and on the development and role of Nordic cooperation.

2. Nordic Cooperation and the "Nordic Model" in Development Cooperation

During the period when the current Nordic Africa policy/strategy documents were being prepared and adopted, in three of the countries – Denmark, Finland and Sweden – the governments were conservative-liberal-centre coalitions, while Norway's government was formed by a coalition of social democrats *(arbeiderpartiet)*, socialist left party *(socialistisk venstre)* and the centre party.

Since the end of the Second World War, a number of more or less ambitious initiatives for closer Nordic cooperation have been launched. Among the main proposals was one for a Nordic Security Pact shortly after the war, while in the 1960s the Nordic governments discussed a plan for a joint Nordic economic organisation, Nordek. Those plans were never implemented, as Finland withdraw in response to pressure from the Soviet Union, and in 1973 Denmark became a member of the then EEC. The only long-lived and still existing institutional structures are the Nordic Council, formed in 1952 and consisting of parliamentarians from all the Nordic countries, and the Nordic Ministers Council, which was formed in 1971 and consists of ten constellations of ministers for various policy areas, including Nordic cooperation.

In recent years, some signs of a revival of "Nordic thinking" can be traced. For instance, in 2009 the Stoltenberg Report was published by the Nordic Council of Foreign Ministers: it suggests ways of strengthening Nordic cooperation in foreign and security policy.[6] In a subsequent meeting among the Nordic ministers of foreign affairs, decisions were made on increased cooperation in a number of foreign and security policy issues, including training in crisis management, international satellite services, cyber security, international criminality and closer cooperation among Nordic embassies on a wide range of issues.[7]

The aim of this section is to establish how Nordic cooperation in relations with Africa has developed in recent years. To a large extent, this implies examining Nordic development cooperation in Africa, as this issue has historically dominated Nordic relations with the continent. One important question in this regard is whether there are signs of strengthened or weakened cooperation, and to identify possible explanatory factors for these trends.

---

6. Stoltenberg, T. (2009). *Nordisk samarbeid om utenriks- og Sikkerhetspolitikk*. Forslag overlevert de nordiske utenriksministere på extraordinärt nordiskt utenriksministermöte. Oslo 9. februar 2009.
7. Declaration from Meeting of the Ministers for Foreign Affairs of the Nordic Countries, Reykjavik, 8–9 June 2009.

The beginning: Nordic joint projects and joint policy initiatives in African countries

In the field of development, Nordic cooperation takes place in many areas and in formal and informal ways. The cooperation on Africa relations is part of a more general cooperation, and often occurs in institutional frameworks that are not aimed only at activities in or together with Africa. Cooperation is sometimes institutionalised among Nordic countries as a group, but often occurs within a broader framework, involving "the like-minded" countries or the Nordic+ group in the development cooperation field, the EU and UN organisations in a large number of policy fields as well as the WTO and the IFIs.

When the "wind of change" swept across Africa 50 and more years ago and the majority of African countries became independent in the late 1950s and early 1960s, the Nordic countries started in a small way to prepare what later became significant development cooperation programmes focused on Africa – in particular the Eastern and Southern (English-speaking) parts of the continent.

During the 1950s, the Nordic countries were newcomers to the aid business and their emerging development aid programmes were mainly channelled through UN agencies. It was not even evident that each of them should build bilateral aid programmes of their own. The option of refraining from bilateral cooperation in favour of joint Nordic projects was informally considered, but discarded.[8] A key argument in favour of joint Nordic efforts was that individual Nordic countries were small and inexperienced in development cooperation and that most of their funding could in the future be expected to be channelled through UN agencies and IFIs.

Based on the thinking of the time, a few joint Nordic projects and programmes were launched. The first was the Scandinavian teaching hospital in South Korea in 1958. In Africa, the Nordic Tanganyika Project in Kibaha, Tanzania, was launched in 1963 and formally handed over to the government of Tanzania in 1970.[9] In 1971, an agreement between the Tanzanian and Nordic governments was signed to establish a joint agricultural training and research project in Mbeya, administered by Finland.

Other examples are the Nordic cooperative projects launched in Tanzania and Kenya in the late 1960s and a large regional agriculture project (MONAP) in Mozambique, starting in 1978 and supported until 1989.[10] The security

---

8. A brief summary of this process is provided in Friis-Bach, J., C. and T. Borring Olesen, S. Kaur-Pedersen and J. Pedersen, 2008. *Idealer og realiteter. Dansk udviklingspolitiks historie 1945–2005.* Köbenhavn: Gyldendal, pp. 29–30.
9. See for instance Billing, A. and C. Carlsson (2008). *Kibaha Education Centre. A sustainable development cooperation project?* Göteborg: University of Göteborg, School of Global Studies.
10. The MONAP project is assessed in SOU 1992:124. *Bistånd under omprövning. Översyn av det svenska utvecklingssamrbetet med Mocambique.*

situation in Mozambique deteriorated during this period, to the detriment of MONAP's activities. In conjunction with their support for MONAP, the Nordic countries prepared a critical joint statement in the first half of the 1980s on the agricultural policy of the Mozambican government.[11]

In Tanzania, Nordic countries in the early 1980s cooperated with the government and the World Bank in an effort to work out an alternative structural adjustment programme in lieu of the adjustments the IMF tried to impose. A programme was designed but was not implemented as agreed and the Tanzania government had to accept the conditions prescribed by the IMF.[12]

Far-reaching Nordic collaboration in development cooperation with Namibia after independence was discussed during the liberation struggle. As early as 1979, a Nordic working group was established to study the conditions and forms of joint Nordic assistance to Namibia when it became independent. Later, the group was dissolved, but in 1988 the Nordic ministers of development cooperation decided to establish a new group to plan and coordinate Nordic assistance to a future independent Namibia. The thought, dating to 1980, that such a Nordic aid programme should be administered by one Nordic country on behalf of all of them was, however, abandoned, so that when Namibia became independent in 1990, each Nordic country established its own bilateral cooperation programme.[13]

In 1986, a joint declaration on expanded economic and cultural cooperation and a framework for cooperation 1986–90 was agreed by the Southern Africa Development Coordination Conference (SADCC) and Nordic countries. The Nordic-SADCC initiative is linked to a proposal by then Finnish Prime Minister Kalevi Sorsa and is sometimes referred to as the Sorsa Initiative.[14] It was seen as an instrument to improve the situation of countries under attack by the apartheid regime in neighbouring South Africa. The cooperation continued after the apartheid system was abandoned and a democratically elected government came to power in 1994. South Africa then became a member of SADCC, which was renamed the Southern Africa Development Community (SADC).

The practical implementation of joint Nordic-funded aid projects was found to be complicated and this form of Nordic cooperation was gradually abandoned

---

11. The MONAP project is summarised in SOU (1992):124. *Bistånd under omprövning. Översyn av det svenska utvecklingssamarbetet med Moçambique.* Stockholm: Allmänna förlaget.
12. Svendsen, K-E. (1986). "The creation of macroeconomic imbalances" in Boesen, J., K. Havnevik, J. Koponen and R. Odgaard (eds), *Tanzania, crisis and struggle for survival.* Uppsala: The Nordic Africa Institute.
13. This process is described in detail in Sellström, T. (2002). *Sweden and National Liberation in Southern Africa. Vol II. Solidarity and Assistance 1970–1994.* Uppsala: The Nordic Africa Institute, pp. 384–9.
14. The Nordic/SADCC Initiative is discussed in Haarlöv, J. (1988). *Regional Cooperation in Southern Africa.* CDR Research Report, no 14. pp. 71–86, and in Tostensen, A, N. Groes, K. Kiljunen and T. Östergaard (1990). *The Nordic/SADCC Initiative: A Nordic Review.* Bergen: Chr. Michelsen Institute.

in favour of other approaches. Regular coordination meetings at the political and professional levels were initiated and some still take place at the political and senior official levels. So-called delegated cooperation, when one country administers also another country's aid programme together with its own in a specific partner country, has been carried out in a few cases. One example is Sweden's administration of the Norwegian support to Mali and Norway's administration of Swedish support to Malawi.

Nordic countries also often cooperate closely in multilateral organisations and the EU, both operationally and politically. The joint Nordic (later Nordic and Baltic countries) executive director posts in the World Bank, the IMF and regional development banks enhance this process. The cooperation in the Nordic Development Fund can also be mentioned in this context, although only part of its lending goes to African countries.

The choice of cooperating countries in Africa by the Nordic countries has been quite similar, and for many years Tanzania and Mozambique have been the top recipients of Nordic aid. They still are, as can be seen from table 2.1, which also includes data for the EC and the EU aggregate. According to the table, 12

Table 2.1. 20 largest sub-Saharan Africa recipient countries in 2008

Denmark	Finland	Norway	Sweden	EC	EU total
1. Tanzania	Tanzania	Tanzania	Tanzania	Ethiopia	Ethiopia
2. Mozamb.	Mozambique	Sudan	Mozambique	Sudan	Mozambique
3. Uganda	Zambia	Mozambique	DRC	Uganda	Tanzania
4. Nigeria	Kenya	Uganda	Kenya	DRC	Sudan
5. Ghana	Ethiopia	Zambia	Sudan	Tanzania	DRC
6. Kenya	South Africa	Malawi	Uganda	South Africa	Uganda
7. Benin	Somalia	Somalia	Zambia	Mozambique	Ghana
8. Burkina F	Sudan	Ethiopia	Ethiopia	Niger	South Africa
9. Sudan	Namibia	DRC	Mali	Mali	Liberia
10. Zambia	DRC	Liberia	Liberia	Chad	Kenya
11. South Afr	Uganda	Burundi	Zimbabwe	Burkina Faso	Burkina Faso
12. Somalia	Chad	Madagascar	Somalia	Côte d'Ivoire	Senegal
13. Zimbabw	CAR	Kenya	Burkina Faso	Madagascar	Botswana
14. Niger	Liberia	Zimbabwe	Malawi	Somalia	Zambia
15. Mali	Angola	South Africa	Rwanda	Senegal	Mali
16. Liberia	Malawi	Angola	South Africa	Malawi	Rep Congo
17. Ethiopia	Sierra Leone	Mali	Chad	Benin	Rwanda
18. DRC	Zimbabwe	Namibia	Burundi	Ghana	Malawi
19. Angola	Rwanda	Eritrea	CAR	Zambia	Somalia
20. Malawi	Nigeria	Nigeria	Equa Guinea	Rwanda	Benin

Sources: EU donor Atlas 2010 and for Norway OECD CRS statistics

of the top 20 receiving countries in Africa are common to all four Nordic countries and an additional four countries are supported by three Nordic countries.

The "Nordic aid model"

Joint Nordic activities were, however, minor compared to the rapidly expanding bilateral programmes that emerged during this period. Some of the features of these bilateral programmes were so similar to each other and sufficiently different from those of "mainstream" DAC members that they were sometimes referred to as the "Nordic model". Some characteristics of this model were:
- Stronger focus on low income countries;
- Stronger support for UN agencies;
- Larger share of grant aid;
- Cooperation programmes over which the receivers had greater influence;
- Clearer distinction between aid and export funding – particularly evident for Norway and Sweden;
- A critical distance from IFIs up to the mid-1980s;
- High ODA/GNI ratio: The Scandinavian countries (Denmark, Norway Sweden) have since the mid-1970s hovered around 1 per cent and together with the Netherlands have always been at the top of the DAC ranking in this field;
- Strong support for the liberation movements in Southern Africa from the late 1960s onwards, transformed into long-term development cooperation when the countries became independent, with the liberation movements now the governments; and,
- "Bridge-builders" between North and South groupings during international negotiations and normative discussions.

Internationally, there is still a tendency to refer to the Nordic countries as a group, and in many international aid or development rankings they form a cluster at the top level.[15] This Nordic aid model, however, gradually eroded from the mid-1980s and the Nordic countries are now moving in different directions, partly following the DAC mainstream.

Membership in the EU by all the countries bar Norway has been one factor in the fading of the Nordic model, but changes in prevailing political and economic thinking, both in the international aid community and in individual Nordic countries, have also played a role. At the same time, the EU is a potential platform for increased Nordic influence. It has also been suggested that the rel-

---

15. One example is the Overall Commitment to Development Index (CDI) 2010, with Sweden and Denmark as number 1 and 2, Norway as number 4 and Finland as number 7. The countries have the same ranking in the commitment to aid index. It can be noted that in the CDI ranking for activities in sub-Saharan Africa, Nordic countries perform more modestly – Overall CDI: Sweden 6, Denmark 7, Norway 8 and Finland 12. Aid CDI: Denmark 2, Sweden 3, Norway 5 and Finland 9.

evance of the Nordic platform may have increased with the enlargement of the EU from 15 to 27 members between 2004 and 2007.[16]

As a non-member of the EU, Norway has since the mid-1990s found other ways to remain relevant. The Norwegian government has facilitated a number of peace negotiations, including those involving Israel-Palestine, Guatemala, Sri Lanka and Sudan. The then Norwegian minister of development cooperation, together with her colleagues from Germany, the UK and the Netherlands formed the Utstein alliance, which worked closely on development policy issues. This alliance represented an inroad into EU aid politics for Norway.

Nordic countries have also been involved in the creation of wider aid coordination platforms, such as the so called Nordic+ group.[17] This group is not tied specifically to Africa, but is used for more general aid policy discussions, in which Africa features largely.

Since the current Norwegian government came to power, Norway has tried to strengthen links with major countries outside the EU, in particular the US, but also with major philanthropic foundations such as the Bill and Melinda Gates Foundation and the big emerging economies. In recent years, Sweden and Denmark have moved closer in their development cooperation thinking, and now form part of a new informal "like-minded" grouping, ideological inclinations different from those of earlier like-minded groupings. As a result of all this, thinking about policy on development cooperation, including Africa policy, is becoming more diverse among the Nordic countries. It is not surprising that the Finnish minister of foreign trade and development in an interview in 2009 lamented that he was "very sad that we have so little Nordic cooperation nowadays".[18]

One field in which the Nordic cooperation seems likely to remain strong, and is in some cases further strengthened, is among the embassies at the operational level in individual cooperating countries. This includes division of labour, delegation of cooperation areas, covering for each other in case of staff vacancies, coordination and cooperation, joint actions in wider local groupings. The level of cooperation and harmonisation depends on many factors, among them the "chemistry" between representatives stationed in the country and the inclusiveness or otherwise of the local EU group. The cooperation among embassies has recently been further strengthened by a decision of the Nordic Council based on the Stoltenberg Report.[19]

---

16. Interview for this study.
17. The Nordic countries, Ireland, the Netherlands and the UK.
18. This was cited in an article headlined "Farewell to the Nordic model", in *Development Today*, no. 21–22, 2010.
19. Stoltenberg, T. (2009). *Nordisk samarbeid om Utenriks- og Sikkerhetspolitikk*.

3. The Aim of the Policy/Strategy Documents and their Overall Design

The Africa policy-guiding documents of the four countries take as their point of departure the rapid economic and social changes in many African countries in recent years, which have given rise to broader contacts with Africa. Domestic economic interests in Nordic countries are more interested in expanding their relations with their African counterparts than they were 10-15 years ago.

The policy-guiding documents reflect general policies in areas such as development cooperation, trade and general foreign policy adjusted for the regional circumstances in Africa. As mentioned earlier, an important aim has been to broaden perspectives beyond development cooperation. The launching of an Africa policy/strategy may, however, also have other motives, as discussed in section 6.

Nordic countries' Africa policies/strategies

The Africa policies/strategies of individual Nordic countries differ in the explicit definition of their own aims and in their outlines.

The preparation process has been different in different countries. In the case of Norway and Finland, a limited number of seminars and other contacts with interest groups outside the ministry and the authorities took place. The perception of civil society organisations is that their influence on the text has been very limited. In Denmark and Sweden, the preparations were more extensive, with background papers commissioned from researchers, consultative meetings and, in the case of Sweden, the opening of a blog for discussion. However, even in these countries at least some civil society representatives felt the impact of their interventions was weak.

While the documents were in preparation, there were some contacts between Nordic countries, but no efforts to work jointly. One example is a seminar at NAI as part of the Swedish preparations, with representatives from other countries invited. The finalised Danish Africa strategy was also presented in Sweden, as part of the preparation of the Swedish document.

However, with Nordic civil society organisations advocating issues considered important to African governments and civil society organisations, they may have had some indirect influence on policy documents, but these influences are difficult to trace and are probably very modest

With one exception, there are no indications that researchers or policymakers in Africa have been seriously consulted in the preparation of this generation of policy-guiding documents. This exception is, of course, The Africa Commission report initiated by the Danish prime minister, with 10 Africans among the 18 commissioners. The secretariat of the Commission recently has moved from the Danish ministry of foreign affairs to the AU office in Addis Ababa. In the case of Sweden, African ambassadors to Sweden were invited to two meetings during the preparation phase.

The main documents to be compared in this study are the Africa policies/strategies. Other documents on relations with Africa and on general development cooperation are, however, occasionally referred to in the text. A brief summary of the documents for each of the four Nordic countries is provided below.

Danish documents

– *Denmark in Africa – A continent on its way. The Government's priorities for Denmark's cooperation with sub-Saharan Africa* (August 2007).
– *Realising the Potential of Africa's Youth. Report of the Africa Commission* (May 2009).
– *Freedom from Poverty, Freedom to Change* (May 2010).

The first document – *Denmark in Africa* – is the most recent Danish Africa strategy and was launched after a new Danish government took power 2007, with increased ODA on the agenda.

According to the strategy, Africa will be the main priority for Denmark's development cooperation in years to come. There will also be an increased and broader political engagement with Africa, in which foreign trade, environmental and security policies will play key roles (*Denmark in Africa*, p. 6).

Denmark in Africa states that poverty reduction will be the foundation of Denmark's engagement in Africa.

The three strategic objectives for Denmark's relations with Africa in 2007–2011 are:
- Inclusion of Africa in globalisation
- Increased regional integration and strengthened cooperation between Africa and the EU.
- More and better assistance for Africa, with the focus on young people, gender equality and, in particular, employment. (ibid., p. 9)

The strategy also emphasises that global issues such as climate change, contagious disease, sustainable use of natural resources, migration and radicalisation are making Africa a more important international player. It is argued that to find sustainable solutions to these global challenges, Africa must be included as an equal partner. Development cooperation is one of the many instruments employed for better integration of Africa into global growth and development.

The second document is the report of the Africa Commission, the commission's co-chairs being the Danish prime minister and the Tanzanian president. It consisted of selected African and Danish policymakers, researchers and representatives from the private sector. The report launches five international initiatives: 1) Benchmarking African Competitiveness; 2) Access to investment finance for small and medium-sized enterprises; 3) Unleashing African entrepreneurship; 4) Access to sustainable energy; and 5) Promoting post-primary education and research. The focus is on the importance of creating employment for the young generation of Africans and the role of entrepreneurship in this process. The initiatives suggested by the commission are in line with and reinforce Danish positions in the Africa strategy. It has also been suggested[20] that establishing the commission was aimed at enhancing the impression that Africa and Denmark have a special relationship.

Freedom from Poverty, Freedom to Change is a new strategy for Danish development cooperation. It was launched in May 2010, three years after the Africa policy. It contains a number of changes in Danish development cooperation policy. One is the stronger emphasis on the link between freedom, identified as individual and political rights, and development. "We should always remember that the purpose of Danish development cooperation is to set people free and thereby enable them to escape poverty. This is the core of the new strategy for Denmark's development cooperation" (p.5). The strategy establishes five political priorities for development cooperation: 1) growth and development; 2) freedom, democracy and human rights; 3) gender equality; 4) stability and fragility; and 5) environment and climate. The document also refers to the recommendations of the Africa Commission on private-sector driven economic growth and employment as a way to escape poverty.

The new strategy for development cooperation will therefore also have an impact on development cooperation with Africa. Thus, there is one general strategy, one regional strategy and an international commission report guiding Denmark's relations with Africa, besides documents covering policy areas other than development cooperation.

In the case of Denmark, the policy shift outlined in the "Freedom Strategy" from 2010 covering development cooperation in general trumps previous Africa policy documents. At the same time, the new approach underscores the growth and employment focus of the Africa Commission report. The three strategic objectives of the Africa strategy remain in focus, while private sector development and global integration of Africa are further enhanced.

Finnish documents

– *Africa in Finnish Development Policy. Finland's development policy framework programme* (July 2009).
– *Africa in Finnish Foreign Policy* (February 2010).
– *Development Policy Programme. Towards a Sustainable and Just World Community.* Government Decision in Principle (2007).

---

20. Interview.

Finland is the only country that has published two parallel Africa policy documents, one called a framework programme with the title *Africa in Finnish Development Policy*, covering only development cooperation, and one with a broader focus, *Africa in Finnish Foreign Policy*, but including development cooperation.

In the case of Finland, the general policy document guiding development cooperation was adopted before the two Africa-related ones. Both the *Development Policy Programme* and the framework programme *Africa in Finnish Development Policy* can be seen as signifying the intention of the new Finnish government that came to power in 2007 to reform development cooperation. The reintroduction of sustainable development as the main objective of development policy is one important facet of this reform and the guiding principles of development policy are stated to be coherence, complementarity and effectiveness.

Africa in Finnish Development Policy can be regarded as further defining the implications of general Finnish development policy in a rapidly changing African context and creating "a strategic framework programme for strengthening partnership between Finland and Africa through development policy measures".[21] It starts with a brief overview of guiding principles for the implementation of the framework programme and then mainly describes ongoing activities and plans for 2009–12.

This framework programme reaffirms that poverty eradication and promoting economically, socially and ecologically sustainable development are the most important objectives of Finland's development policy. These key objectives are in line with the UN Millennium Development Goals.

In accordance with Finland's general development cooperation programme, the framework for Africa emphasises the importance of climate and environmental issues as well as the prevention and management of crises and support for peace processes. Greater significance than hitherto is afforded the private sector and trade as an engine for economic development.

The document stresses that improvement in the position of women and girls and promotion of gender equity and equality within society, and improvement in the situation of vulnerable or marginalised groups are central prerequisites for sustainable growth in Africa. The struggle against HIV/AIDS as a societal problem is a very important development challenge in many African countries. These objectives are promoted in all Finnish development policy documents and therefore influence policy towards Africa (*Africa in Finnish Development Policy*, pp. 12–15).

Africa in Finnish Foreign Policy lists a number of objectives in four policy areas: 1) Security and the political situation, including crisis management, prevention and mediation, human rights, democracy and good governance, Africa

---

21. From the foreword of *Africa in Finnish Development Policy*.

in EU foreign and security policy, and Africa and the UN Security Council; 2) Development cooperation; 3) Trade and economic relations; and 4) Cooperation structures of the EU and Africa. The document concludes that all segments of foreign policy must serve the same foreign policy goals and stresses the need for greater consistency between activities on different levels, for instance in bilateral relations, when influencing EU policy and in multilateral organisations.

It also notes that Finland should engage in closer, more versatile and more equal dialogue with Africa. Such dialogue should cover global issues, including climate change, weapons control, disarmament and human rights.

The document sees as a particular need consideration of how Finland could more actively promote peace and security in Africa, including more flexible funding arrangements involving sources other than development cooperation funds.

Economic growth is viewed as one of the prerequisites for African development, with trade at its centre. Finland supports the development of Africa's own trade capacity and promotes Finnish trade and economic relations with Africa.

According to the document, Finland is also well qualified to act as a bridge builder and supports stronger representation of the African continent on the Security Council as part of the ongoing reform process of the UN.

Promoting Africa's own integration is another of Finland's key goals. In particular, Finland supports the capacity of the AU and other regional organisations to solve political and military conflicts and crises (*Africa in Finnish Foreign Policy*, pp. 76–8).

The Norwegian documents

– *Africa Strategy. Platform for an Integrated Africa Policy* (December 2008).
– *Climate, Conflict and Change. Norwegian development policy adapting to change.* Government Report no. 13 (2008–09) to parliament.

Norway calls its strategy *Platform for an Integrated Africa Policy*. The aim of the Platform is to give a general idea of Norwegian cooperation with Africa in various policy areas, and to provide a basis for devising and implementing concrete measures.

According to the platform, the sustainable use and management of the world's resources is an overriding aim of Norwegian foreign and international development policy. The government is seeking an integrated approach towards Africa that takes into account and mutually reinforces foreign policy, development policy, security policy, environment policy and trade and industry policy. Africa's progress in recent years has provided real opportunities for broader co-operation with African countries in all these areas

The platform emphasises that vital to Africa's growth and prosperity is the sustainable exploitation of raw materials such as oil, minerals and timber and the equitable distribution of revenues. Norway therefore seeks to support African countries in strengthening their own revenue base by developing sound and transparent administrative procedures, effective taxation systems and by reducing illicit financial flows. This will ensure that Africa's rich resources benefit the whole population and contribute to lasting development and poverty reduction.

Although Norway's relations with sub-Saharan Africa have traditionally been linked to development assistance and missionary work, cooperation is constantly being expanded into other areas. According to the platform, Norway has entered into political dialogue with several African countries on foreign policy themes such as peace and conflict resolution, health and environmental issues.

The government report to parliament entitled *Climate, Conflict and Capital. Norwegian development policy adapting to change* is a general policy document and therefore one level above the Africa platform in the hierarchy of policy documents. It specifies the features of Norwegian development policy in a wide sense, under seven headings: national responsibilities of the partner state, global framework, climate change, conflicts and fragile states, capital flows in and out of poor countries, actors and areas and coherence between domestic and development policy. It moves the focus from traditional bilateral development cooperation with a select number of partner countries to thematically focused support for international initiatives – sometimes initiated by Norway – to address identified global development challenges. The document signals an important change in the thrust of Norwegian development cooperation.

Many of these changes are also reflected in the Africa platform, prepared more or less simultaneously. The two documents are thus compatible, although *Climate, Conflict and Capital* seems to have made a stronger impact and contains more clearly defined strategies for the ongoing shift in Norwegian development cooperation from traditional bilateral engagement to supporting global and international thematic initiatives and programmes.

Swedish documents

- *Sweden and Africa – a policy to address common challenges and opportunities* (March 2008).
- *Shared Responsibility. Sweden's Policy for Global Development.* Government bill 2002/03:122.
- *Global Challenges – Our Responsibility.* Government Communication 2007/2008:89.

Sweden's Africa policy's point of departure is *Sweden's Policy for Global Development*, aimed at promoting equitable and sustainable global development. The government communication, *Global Challenges – Our Responsibility*, was presented to parliament at more or less the same time as the Africa policy. This document amounts to a reformed *Policy for Global Development* and should therefore be regarded as the general policy framework for Africa policy.

In *Sweden and Africa,* three aims of Swedish policy are formulated:
- Supporting the countries of Africa and their inhabitants in their efforts to foster peace, democracy and respect for human rights and in relation to economic, social and environmental sustainable development;
- Helping Africa achieve full and active participation in global economic and political cooperation on common challenges; and
- Broadening areas of contact between Sweden and Africa and thereby promoting Swedish and African interests.

The second and third aims are similar to the overall objectives in the Danish document. The Swedish Africa policy then lists eight priority areas and underlines that three of the thematic priorities in the *Policy for Global Development* – climate, democracy and gender equality – enjoy the same salience in the Africa document. Another important aim of this document is to reach beyond development cooperation in relations with African countries, an aim that is also in line with the coherence principle in the *Policy for Global Development*.

As in the Danish Africa strategy, the Swedish document sets out an extensive list of intentions to serve as priorities for implementation. Seven main areas of cooperation between Sweden and Africa are discussed: 1) Growth for poverty reduction and sustainable development, 2) Peace and security in a new regional context, 3) Democracy and human rights – development opportunities, 4) Gender equality – development on the same terms, 5) Environment and climate – national, regional and global; 6) Development opportunities for the individual, including health, education, migration and culture; and 7) Trade and economic cooperation.

The Government bill to which the Africa policy refers, *Shared Responsibility. Sweden's Policy for Global Development,* was adopted by the Swedish government in 2003. It sets out a policy for global development with the overall goal of contributing to equitable and sustainable development. This goal is to apply to all policy areas in a coherent manner. The *Policy for Global Development* is intended to contribute to the achievement of the UN Millennium Declaration and the MDGs and be based on a rights perspective of development.

Global Challenges – Our Responsibility, the government communication on Sweden's policy for global development was presented to parliament in March 2008. As noted above, it reformed *Policy for Global Development*. It defines six global challenges: 1) oppression, 2) economic exclusion, 3) migration flows, 4) climate change and environmental impacts, 5) conflicts and fragile situations and 6) communicable diseases and other health threats. For each of these global challenges, three focus areas are identified. It can be assumed that this perspective, together with an increased focus on support for private sector development, actor-driven cooperation and topic areas in which there is Swedish "value added" will significantly influence Swedish relations and cooperation with Africa.

At a policy level, both the Africa policy and the *Policy for Global Development* documents aim at broadening Swedish relations with African countries beyond traditional development cooperation. Even so, long-term bilateral development cooperation and support for fragile, conflict and post-conflict African states remain the main activities.

***

The fact that the Africa documents of the four countries are designed differently does not necessarily affect their degree of influence on operations in various policy fields, as *realpolitik* and other policy documents sometimes have a larger impact. In the concluding section, the relative influence of Africa policies/strategies compared to general polices, political changes in African and Nordic countries, international trends and other factors are further discussed.

4. Issue Areas Compared

This section compares a number of issue areas based on the formulations in the Africa policy-guiding documents and on experiences in a number of partner countries. The parallel reading of the former reveals striking similarities in some traditionally common Nordic priority areas, but also some areas in which the pattern is more differentiated. In selecting the issue areas, the role they have played in discussions of overall development policy in Nordic countries has been taken into consideration, as has the recentness of their becoming part of this discussion. Altogether 11 issue areas are addressed. They are complemented by a consideration of two features of Nordic development cooperation.

4.1. Importance of coherence

Both the Africa documents and, even more so, the general policy documents on development cooperation emphasise the importance of a coherent policy towards Africa: all relevant policy areas should be coherent or at least not mutually incompatible. This approach is also consistent with EU policy. In the African context, the focus is on coherence between development and security and conflict prevention, migration, foreign trade and climate, but also infectious diseases.

Sweden, with its *Policy for Global Development* from 2003, can be regarded as a Nordic frontrunner on coherence. At the policy level, the importance of coherence and addressing conflicts between various policy areas in a transparent and constructive way is, however, increasingly acknowledged, and not only by the Nordic countries. However, as the experience of the EC and individual EU members with coherence ambitions shows, the challenges to achieving development coherence are great and some competing interests are hard to balance.

The instruments and processes needed to achieve coherence take time to establish, as Sweden has experienced in recent years. Nonetheless, Sweden seems to be in the lead when it comes to organising and monitoring a coherent policy, although much remains to be done. The latest DAC peer review of Sweden (from 2009) raised concerns about the limited staff capacity assigned to this task by the Swedish government and the delay in defining the indicators against which progress in the field of coherence can be measured.[22]

None of the documents reviewed discusses how to handle conflicting interests between different policy areas. One obvious example is humanitarian and development interests versus foreign trade interests in the case of weapons exports. Another issue is determining from which budget line certain activities in the "grey zone" between policy interests are to be financed. The use of military personnel for humanitarian or development activities, such as constructing

---

22. OECD/DAC 2009. *Peer Review Sweden*, chapter 2, pp. 33–41.

wells or schools, is one typical example. Another is funding the costs for receiving immigrants from Nordic development cooperation partner countries. The Norwegian document *Climate, Conflict and Capital* is the only document to mention the issue of which budget line should be used in funding these types of expenditure (p. 7).

While the rhetoric on coherence is strong, the execution is sometimes weak, for various reasons. For instance, Swedish civil society organisations strongly criticise the incoherence between Swedish arms exports to countries like Pakistan in parallel with humanitarian and development aid. Similarly, the Danish parliament recently agreed to provide ODA funds for an initiative under Denmark's defence policy, and according to a Reality of Aid report the trend of using Danish aid for national security purposes is likely to be grow.[23] In Norway, development researchers and civil society organisations have criticised the use of aid money to promote export and trade interests, rather than adjusting trade and trade policy to optimise development effects. In such cases, the direction of coherence is reversed – from development to defence instead of from defence to development – although the borderline between the two areas is difficult to define.

4.2. Private sector development and trade as engine of economic growth

In their Africa policy-guiding documents, all four countries emphasise development of the private sector as an instrument for increased growth, which in turn will reduce poverty. This is also in line with current thinking in international aid circles.

The documents suggest enhanced efforts to include companies from the respective Nordic countries in development cooperation, mixed with promotion of Nordic countries' private sector interests in Africa. This also reflects a broader international trend, emerging from the renewed interest in investment in and trade with Africa. Within development cooperation, all four countries have launched new instruments to support private sector development and promote business interests, and funding of existing instruments has increased,[24] including the equity capital funds established with funding from aid budgets.[25]

Regarding foreign trade, the documents argue there is an urgent need to finalise the EPA negotiations between the EU and ACP countries and for the EU

---

23. Gregersen, L.L., Concord –Denmark (2010). "Diminishing Danish Aid?" in *Reality of Aid 2010 Report*, p. 203.
24. In the case of Finland, this is discussed in Toikka, M. (2010). "Finnish Development Cooperation: A Shift Towards More Donor-Driven Aid?" in *Reality of Aid 2010 Report*, pp. 211-12.
25. For a recent brief overview, see "From export subsidies to investment, vested interests remains" in *Development Today*, no. 21-22, 2010.

to inject new energy into the WTO Doha Round negotiations. Here there is a clear difference between Sweden and Denmark. Sweden does not seem to recognise the concerns of many African governments and civil society organisations in Africa and Europe in the same way as Denmark, which qualified its approach with conditions reflecting those concerns.[26] Sweden also differs from Norway in its uncritical view on general trade liberalisation and the inclusion of TRIPS issues. This is one policy area, according to the Africa policy-guiding documents, where Sweden's position is somewhat special in the Nordic context.

4.3. Peace and security

The security-development nexus has been high on the international development agenda since the early 1990s. The policy documents of all four Nordic countries view armed conflicts and crisis as both security and development obstacles. From a development perspective, conflict prevention and conflict mitigation are crucial.

A common feature of all four countries is the preparedness to support African security institutions with both military and civil resources. The three Nordic EU members emphasise their willingness to contribute to EU peacekeeping initiatives. All four recognise the importance of UN security institutions and are committed to supporting UN and African peacekeeping efforts both financially and militarily. NEPAD's APRM is also identified as an important African institution to be supported.

At the bilateral level, Norway and Finland mention initiatives to train police and the military in cooperating countries. Strong support for post-conflict states is emphasised. The situation of women and children in conflict and post-conflict situations is also stressed. Finland also offers itself as a forum for negotiations and conflict-solving activities.

Support on security issues is often related to support for regional integration and for various African regional organisations. This is also in line with the Joint EU-Africa Strategy.

Although individual Nordic countries mention slightly different initiatives in their documents, they are obviously agreed on strong support for this policy area, in that they commit themselves to providing support at international, regional and national levels, including providing military resources.

4.4. Democracy and human rights

There is also strong commitment to democracy and human rights in the documents of all four countries. This issue has been strongly promoted since the early 1990s, and has in principle been one of the main objectives since the Nordic

---

26. *Denmark in Africa – A continent on its way*, p. 24.

countries began their bilateral development cooperation. Special efforts are suggested in support of democracy and human rights as part of tackling the challenges of fragile states.

The similarities between all four Nordic countries in this policy area are among the strongest, and the issues pointed out as suitable for support are very similar. The role of the AU and other African organisations in improving democracy and human rights is stressed and commitments to support these activities are made.

Among the suggested approaches to supporting democracy and human rights is convincing African countries to join the African Peer Review Mechanism (APRM) within NEPAD, involving NGOs in advocacy and service delivery and strengthening national systems and institutions that promote democracy and fight corruption. With regard to the latter, Norway and Sweden explicitly commit themselves to zero tolerance. The challenges in implementing policy goals in this area are significant. Aid statistics from Nordic countries show that in recent years a larger share has been channelled for these purposes, although the amount differs significantly from year to year.

4.5. Gender equality and the role of women

Gender equality has long been a common development commitment by all Nordic countries, as is visible in the Africa policy-guiding documents. The link between enabling women to participate in political and economic life and increased economic growth is emphasised in all documents. As *Denmark in Africa* expresses it: "women must be included if Africa is to significantly reduce poverty and create the necessary growth" (p. 40). Gender equality is thus considered both a goal in itself and a means of improving aid effectiveness and sustainable development.

Besides general statements on gender equality, the Africa documents, with slight variation, underline the importance of measures to implement the gender equality goals that they will introduce or further strengthen, such as increasing women's participation in political life and in business development and trade, convincing African decision-makers to stop female genital mutilation and promoting women's right to control their own bodies and to freedom from violence and sexual abuse.

All these measures on gender equality are well-known from previous Nordic policy documents, and reflect the objectives of the general development cooperation policy documents.

4.6. Regional integration in Africa

Support for regional integration in Africa has long been part of the Nordic countries' development cooperation programmes, with SADCC/SADC cooperation in Southern Africa from 1980 a main component. The EU membership of three of the Nordic countries and the increased focus on security issues have over time further enhanced the regional perspective, and this is evident in the current Africa policy/strategy documents. Some of these issues have already been dealt with in the section on security.

Judging from the Africa policy-guiding documents, support for regional African organisations will continue and be enhanced, in particular in the field of peace and security, but also in the trade sector, partly linked to the EPA process the EU is pushing.

The AU seems at present to be the most popular African organisation among the Nordic countries. The AU is the counterpart to the EU in the Joint EU-Africa Strategy. There are great hopes in the EU that the AU will emerge as an important African player, able to take responsibility for security and conflict issues with material and financial support from the EU and bilaterally. The Norwegian platform states that the "AU could become the most important peace and security actor in Africa" (p. 20) and the other countries have similar formulations in their documents.

The third summit on the Joint EU-Africa Strategy in late November 2010 resulted in a Tripoli Declaration and the adoption of a new action plan for 2011-13. The action plan is based on all the existing eight partnerships, while experiences with the first action plan suggest a reduction in the number of partnerships to make the activities more effective. The Tripoli Declaration also contains a commitment to conclude the EPAs, implying continuation of the negotiations that have dragged on for a long time.

The NEPAD initiative, which in the 1990s was a favourite among many donors, including the Nordics, is now a more modest recipient of regional aid. Most attention is given to the APRM instrument for peer reviewing of the governance of individual African states. With the weak performance of SADC during recent years, the interest of the Nordics has gradually diminished.

A new Swedish strategy for regional cooperation with sub-Saharan Africa 2010–15 was launched in December 2010. It is based on the *Policy for Global Development* and the Swedish Africa policy. The focus is building the capacity of regional organisations, mainly the AU and regional economic organisations, in particular the East African Community. Priority policy areas are peace and security, environment and climate and economic integration. This is also in line with EU policy.

The issue of how to reduce and handle the EPAs' possibly distorting effects on regional integration in Africa is not discussed in the Africa documents, despite its importance in international debate. The link between trade discussions, in which EPAs bulk large, and the regional integration discussions, from which EPAs are almost absent, thus seems to have been neglected.

4.7. Inclusion of Africa in the globalising world

International interest in further integrating Africa into the global economy has increased concurrently with the intensified competition for the continent's raw materials, its higher economic growth and its improved governance. This interest is apparent in the international donor community, including the Nordic countries. The issue is also linked to private sector development and trade. It should be noted, however, that views on how such an inclusion should be effected vary widely.

The Nordic countries have perspectives similar to those of other OECD countries, although, for instance, some of Norway's initiatives regarding oil for development, continental shelf protection and coastal zone management can be interpreted as efforts to strengthen Africa's position in international negotiations and its capacity to protect its natural resources in those negotiations. As already mentioned, support for increased involvement of Africa in globalisation and improving the capacity of African countries and organisations in international organisations and negotiations is one of three strategic objectives in both the Danish and the Swedish Africa policy/strategy documents.

Denmark most explicitly expresses support for stronger representation for Africa in the UN Security Council and improved cooperation between the UN, AU and EU. This issue is also mentioned in the Finnish and Swedish documents, but is not as strongly worded. The Norwegian platform is the only document to explicitly state that the poorest countries should gain greater influence in the World Bank and IMF and that privatisation and liberalisation of public services should not be set as conditions for assistance (p.20).

Among the intentions of the Swedish government are:
- promoting open trade, including increased participation in international trade and greater access to EU markets for African countries, support for wider African membership of the WTO and encouraging greater exchanges between African countries and the OECD;
- supporting African efforts to achieve better trade terms and conditions, regional integration and harmonisation, a better investment climate, enhanced production capacity, diversification and reduced dependence on raw materials; and
- encouraging development of other conditions for economic growth and participation in the global economy

While Norway has a number of initiatives aimed at improving the capacity of African countries to defend their national interests, the other Nordic countries commit themselves in more general terms to supporting Africa's efforts to increase its role in international organisations.

In the case of Denmark, broader dialogue at all levels, closer research exchanges, support for dealing with the repercussions of climate change and addressing the fundamental reasons for forced migration are mentioned as important issue areas.

Actions by Nordic countries to strengthen the capacity of African countries to participate in international negotiations may be welcomed by African governments. Implementing such actions may also be combined with promoting the commercial activities of Nordic companies in Africa.

4.8. Climate adjustment and environmental sustainability in Africa

Efforts to constrain global warming and to adjust to the effects of this process have in recent years become increasingly important in the international community. The Copenhagen climate summit in December 2009 was a disappointment for most participants and observers. The Copenhagen Accord was not legally binding and did not commit countries to a binding successor to the Kyoto protocol. On funding, a non-binding commitment was included by the developed countries to raise US$30 billion of "new and additional resources" from 2010–12. At the subsequent climate change conference in Cancun in December 2010, the Copenhagen Accord was accepted and some modest steps towards a post-Kyoto agreement were taken. The Cancun agreement included a green climate fund, proposed to be worth US$100 billion a year by 2020, to assist poor countries in financing emissions reductions and other adaptations, but no agreement was reached on how the money would be raised.

The Africa documents were launched before the Copenhagen summit, but climate issues were prominent in all of them, but with slightly different accentuation. Norway has so far launched the most initiatives, including mitigation of climate change and clean energy measures in Africa. The most visible of these is the international climate and forest initiative. In an attempt to ensure that international initiatives in Africa focus more on the climate dimensions, an International Commission on Climate Change and Development was established through a Swedish initiative. Its report, *Closing the Gaps,* was published in 2009.

Many resources for climate mitigation and adjustment will be channelled through international climate funds, although so far the amounts disbursed fall far short of what was pledged. There are few examples of commitments by richer countries to fund climate adjustment in poor countries from sources other than their aid budgets. Instead, climate adjustment activities have normally been included as part of development cooperation.[27] This issue is not reflected in the Africa policy documents.

---

27. In the case of Sweden, SEK 4 billion was earmarked in 2008 for this purpose over a three year period.

4.9. Migration

Migration into Europe from war-torn and fragile countries is seen as a threat by the EU and its member states, including the Nordics. Among them, the strongest domestic political pressure to reduce immigration exists in Denmark, and therefore also strong political pressure to include disincentives to emigration from Africa. Against this background, it is not surprising that tackling the fundamental reasons for forced migration is one of the three main objectives of Denmark's Africa strategy. Sweden seems to be following Denmark on this issue, and migration flows is one of three issue areas listed in *Global Challenges – Our Responsibility*, the government communication from 2008 on how to handle the global challenge of economic exclusion. This aim is also behind the three Nordic EU members' strong support for the ongoing integration of migration issues into EU cooperation with Africa. Support for African countries interested in introducing and implementing national legislation on this matter is increasing in the EU.

Table 4.1 shows the increased funding of migration costs from the aid budgets of the Nordic countries in recent years.

Table 4.1. ODA costs for refugees in donor countries 2005–08 (US$ million)

Country	2005	2006	2007	2008
Denmark	70	42	45	49
Finland	17	11	18	26
Norway	68	67	78	141
Sweden	143	164	258	375

Source: OECD/DAC: Development Cooperation Report 2010

4.10. New actors in Africa

Finland mentions relations with China and India as a strategic factor in one of its Africa documents (*Africa in Finnish Foreign Policy*), which has a rather detailed section on this issue, ending with three Finnish objectives.

- Dialogue on Africa with the emerging economic powers needs to be increased, including on development policy. The EC initiative to start tripartite cooperation and dialogue is a step in the right direction. The dialogue with emerging donors should also include the expert level and unofficial actors (the so-called track-two actors);
- In the dialogue, it must be possible to discuss human rights and good governance as well as issues such and peace and security; and
- Finland keeps questions related to Africa on the agenda in its bilateral relations with China and also in EU-China relations. Finland aims at always including a paragraph on common efforts related to Africa in the final documents of EU-China summits (*Africa in Finnish Foreign Policy*, pp. 15–16).

In the government communication on Sweden's Africa policy it is stated:
> Africa's growth potential and abundance of natural resources is drawing an increasingly wide response from the surrounding world. This growing interest is exemplified by China's involvement in Africa. However, India, Brazil and other countries in the South are also stepping up their activities on the continent. Investment, credit and the export of African natural resources have given a major stimulus to African development, and often include third country support for the development of African infrastructure. (*Sweden and Africa*, pp. 6–7)

The communication points out the risk in countries deriving large export incomes from resource exploitation that profits will be concentrated in the hands of the few. If growth is to contribute to sustainable development, it must be broad-based, encompass all aspects of social development and benefit the poor to a greater extent than at present (pp. 6–7).

When the communication later provides points of departure for Swedish positions and policy, it states that consideration should also be given to these new actors in Africa. Their relations with Africa and collaboration with and within multilateral organisations will have an impact on Sweden's Africa policy (p. 27).

Among the general policy documents on development cooperation, Denmark's *Freedom from Poverty, Freedom to Change* strategy and Norway's *Climate, Conflict and Capital* document contain quite elaborate discussions on this issue. The Norwegian report warns that if global organisations fail to strengthen the emerging powers' role in them and increase their relevance, there is a real risk developing countries will not consider them to have value, which could lead to the emergence of competing organisations. On a similar note, *Freedom from Poverty* states that Denmark will strive to ensure that new actors assume the obligations associated with multilateral cooperation (p.10).

The Danish Africa strategy states:
> In recent years, a number of donors outside the traditional OECD donor circle have begun to make their presence felt in Africa. This applies in particular to China, which has promised to double its assistance to Africa by 2009. This is a positive development that should be welcomed. At the same time it is important that the African countries ensure that new development assistance partners support a development process that promotes democracy and human rights as well as sustainable utilisation of natural resources. (p. 32)

4.11. Joint EU-Africa Strategy and EU as a guiding example

The three Nordic countries that are members of the EU all put strong emphasis on the Joint EU-Africa Strategy, making it a centrepiece for them to relate to.

They also stress the importance of influencing EU policy towards Africa, which provides stronger leverage than their own bilateral interventions.

Regarding development cooperation, Denmark's position is that it is more important to influence the EU than to let the EU harmonise Denmark with other EU countries. Swedish Africa policy also emphasises the possibility of influencing common EU policy. It seems Finland is most open to influence by the EU. Finland has also chosen four of the eight Africa-EU partnerships to enhance the effectiveness of its contributions. They are peace and security, democratic governance and human rights, climate change and science and information.

As mentioned earlier, the Swedish Africa policy in support of EPA negotiations is not qualified, while Denmark argues for those negotiations to be finalised but with a number of amendments to the content, obviously in response to African and civil society representations.

4.12. Value added – comparative advantages

The comparative advantage and value added issues are highlighted by all four countries. Three sectors are common in the Danish, Norwegian and Swedish lists: energy, environment and health. Norway's platform stands out in mentioning a number of more specific areas, namely petroleum management, fisheries, coastal zone management, power supply and road and bridge construction. Denmark is the only country to mention the business sector in this context, although all the countries prioritise private sector development as the main instrument for promoting economic growth. Sweden also mentions telecom and agriculture as particularly competitive branches. Finland does not specify particular areas, but underlines the principle of focusing on sectors in which Finland can provide added value.

The emphasis on value added or comparative advantage is associated with a stronger supply-side perspective, which may also have export-promotion effects. In this context, it should be noted that it is sometimes challenging to reconcile giving priority to areas in which a country assesses it can provide value added with the Paris Declaration commitment to safeguard the ownership of the receiving partner country.

4.13. Nordic-Africa annual informal foreign ministry meetings

Nordic countries often claim that due to their support for African liberation movements during the 1970s and 1980s, a special relationship exists between them and at least the countries and governments of Southern Africa. In official speeches, this link is often referred to by both parties. But this was more than 20 years ago, and new generations of politicians and public officials have arisen. So how much of a special link survives? Quite clearly, less than is assumed in official speeches. However, there may still be situations where Nordic and African countries more easily find common ground.

As the foreign ministers' meetings are informal, there are no protocols or resolutions. On the other hand, the informality makes them useful for networking and shaping relations that may facilitate closer cooperation between Nordic and African countries under more formal circumstances.

According to staff in the Africa departments of all four countries, the meetings have improved mutual understanding of Nordic and African thinking on many important issues and facilitated relations between the parties, including during more formal international negotiations, when, for instance, African and EU countries in principle work as groups.

After a couple of years, African countries noted that Nordic countries were not represented at a high enough level and that some of the energy of the meetings had evaporated. However, this has again changed, and both African and Nordic foreign ministers have reportedly been satisfied with the outcome of the most recent meetings.[28] In recent years, the meetings have been forums for discussion of and cooperation on various global public goods, such as climate change and security, and it is reported that more controversial issues have also been raised.

In the interviews, it was noted that Africa-Nordic relations are more important today as a result of the increased importance of Africa in the global economy and politically, particularly when it comes to addressing global public goods. It was reported that African participants also appreciate the meetings as a platform to discuss global issues, such as the financial crisis, climate, energy and not just the usual governance and domestic problems.

4.14. Monitoring

Despite general statements on the importance of results-based management, etc., no Nordic country includes a special mechanism to monitor or evaluate the implementation of its Africa policy/strategy. This may seem somewhat astonishing, particularly in the case of Sweden, as the Swedish government strongly emphasises serious monitoring and results-based development cooperation. The attitude to monitoring may be related to the importance attached to the Africa documents compared to other documents that guide policy.

Thus, African policies/strategies seem to be launched without defining which major results should be reached by the end of the term of the strategy. To work out a strategy without making it possible to follow up on its results seems to be less than constructive.

One explanation may be that the aim of Africa policy/strategy documents

---

28. This was mentioned by a number of the interviewees.

is at least partly symbolic: to show that a government, by producing a policy document, is aware of developments in a region and wants to act. The aim may also be to prevent the perception that Africa and a country's relations with that continent have been forgotten in a stream of actions and media coverage focusing on other geographical areas.[29] If this is the case, then monitoring may be considered less important.

---

29. Suggestions by interviewees.

5. Special Features of the Africa Policies of Individual Nordic Countries

We now turn to summarise the areas in which features special to individual Nordic countries can be identified.

Most of the strong similarities among the Nordic countries in their development policies towards Africa discussed above reflect common general priorities and are not specific to their relations with Africa.

The large share of their aid that has historically been allocated to Africa is one indicator of the high priority this continent has had in their bilateral development cooperation policies. Budget figures from 2009 onwards indicate that we may see Africa's share of total ODA declining. This is most evident in the case of Norway. This is not because the large share of geographically defined bilateral aid allocated Africa is shrinking, but because total geographically defined bilateral aid is declining while the share of funds earmarked for global or national programmes and initiatives is increasing.

There are a number of common traditional Nordic aid priorities in the field of development cooperation in the Africa policy-guiding documents, among them democracy, human rights, gender issues, environment, peace and security and regional integration. Similarities in other thematic areas between Nordic countries also exist, but reflect the fact that the Nordics are following current international trends. Examples are private sector development as the main driver of economic growth, support for adaptation to climate change and cooperation in the field of migration.

The efforts to integrate African countries into a globalising world can also be seen as a means to include Nordic countries in the ongoing international race for African natural resources. This aspect is most apparent in the case of Norway. However, there is no significant indication that the Nordic countries are increasing their share of trade and investment in Africa, or that sub-Saharan Africa's share of their total trade and FDI is increasing, with Norway the exception for FDI (tables 1.1–1.3).[30]

Apart from the many similarities, some special features in the Africa documents of the individual Nordic countries can be identified. Many of these are not specific to Africa policies, but reflect differences in each country's general development policies. This trend is even more evident in the most recent development policy documents, including the annual budget bills of the Nordic countries, than in their current Africa policy documents.

Summarised below are some of the most evident special features of individual Nordic countries.

---

30. Data on Nordic imports from sub-Saharan Africa do not include crude oil, which is normally refined in other countries before being shipped to the Nordics. Given this, import values should probably be higher.

Denmark

Denmark's development cooperation policy has from the outset had two main motives, solidarity and enlightened self-interest, and two main objectives, poverty reduction and involving Denmark's private sector, which can also be expressed as promoting the private sector's search for international markets. The current changes in Africa enhance the prospects for this "two leg strategy" and recent developments in many African countries certainly provide more openings for achieving the second objective.

Some special features of Danish Africa policy are:
- Strong focus on concentrating long-term bilateral development cooperation on fewer countries and on fewer sectors and programmes within each cooperating country. Since *Denmark in Africa* was published, the Danish government has decided to reduce the number of long-term partner countries from 26 to 15. By January 2011, seven of the countries to be phased out had been selected, of which two are in Africa – Benin and Zambia.
- The Africa Commission Report is a unique feature, giving Denmark international recognition and important inputs into its development policy. The strongest impact so far has been the emphasis on youth employment and the general improvement of the situation for youth. In development cooperation, Denmark places stronger emphasis than other countries on the large youth cohorts in Africa and the importance of creating jobs suitable for young people and improving education and skills training. This is also the main focus of the Africa Commission Report.
- New instruments supporting efforts by the Danish private sector to increase its engagement in Africa, one of the objectives of the Africa strategy, have been put in place. Contradicting this trend, Denmark has in recent years channelled surpluses from the IFU into the state budget, while other Nordic countries have provided new funding to their corresponding equity funds.
- Priority for sectors and issue areas in which Danish competence is competitive.
- Support for the EPA process, but with explicit conditions on issues such as the exclusion of Singapore, no EU-specific interests with regard to market access, EU to phase out its trade-distorting agricultural subsidies, etc. *Denmark in Africa* acknowledges many of the concerns of African governments and African and European civil society representatives on the content of EPAs and the process so far. Denmark thus argues for significant changes in the EU's approach in the EPA negotiations (*Denmark in Africa*, pp. 23–4).
- *Denmark in Africa* is the policy document most explicit in supporting stronger African representation on the Security Council and closer cooperation between the UN, the AU and EU. As in the other Nordic countries' Africa documents, security policy is the focus here.

- Strong emphasis on migration issues. Denmark is the only Nordic country to have decided to cut aid as a lever to push countries receiving Danish aid to accept the repatriation of asylum seekers from those countries. This arises from a decision of 2003, the result of an agreement between the government and the populist right-wing Danish People's Party.
- Of the Nordic countries, Denmark has the highest share of total ODA and bilateral ODA going to Africa
- It is also the only country with an upper limit on the aid budget volume, pegged at the same absolute level for the period 2011–14.
- Priority allocation of climate-related aid as adjustment schemes in bilateral programmes, rather than to international climate funds.

Finland

- *Africa in Finnish Development Policy* is the only Africa document dealing with development cooperation issues, while broader relations outside development cooperation are covered in *Africa in Finnish Foreign Policy*. Finland is thus the only Nordic country with two parallel Africa policy documents.
- Of the Nordic policy documents, *Africa in Finnish Development Policy* stands out as the most "traditional" development policy, with long-term bilateral and regional development cooperation programmes at its core. The document is also more process-oriented than the corresponding ones from the other three countries. One major feature of *Africa in Finnish Development Policy* is the "Back to Rio" perspective, intended to restore sustainable development as the central issue of development. Economic growth, it is stressed, must be environmentally, climatically and socially sustainable, while the eradication of poverty in line with the MDGs is a primary development objective. This is also the only Africa policy document in which current traditional bilateral country and regional cooperation programmes form a main part of the text.
- A common feature in both Finnish documents is the priority afforded areas and branches where Finnish knowledge and companies are internationally competitive, without being specific. Linked to this is the promotion of the private sector as an instrument for increasing economic growth through new mechanism such as the Finn Partnership, a fund providing seed money to smaller Finnish companies.
- Very strong support for the AU and the Joint EU-Africa Strategy is expressed, as is strong support for regional cooperation in Africa. The EU links are strongly emphasised by Finland. While the policy documents of all four Nordic Africa countries stress the importance of the AU and support for its capacity building, the Finnish framework programme is the strongest on this point and in supporting the Joint EU-Africa Strategy, the Cotonou Agreement and the EPAs.

- *Africa in Finnish Foreign Policy* underscores the importance of policy coherence with respect to development cooperation, trade policy, environment and climate policy. The basic premise is that all elements of Finland's foreign policy – foreign and security policy, development policy and development cooperation as well as trade policy – should serve the same foreign policy goals.

In sum, what emerges is a Finnish document on development cooperation with Africa that attempts to combine bilateral and regional cooperation based on sustainable development and MDG-based poverty reduction with a focus on sectors and branches in which Finnish knowledge and commercial interests are internationally competitive. It is also strongly framed within the Joint EU-Africa Strategy. The *Africa in Finnish Foreign Policy* document, with its emphasises on overall policy coherence in order to serve foreign policy goals, implies a politicising of development cooperation. In the Finland-Africa context, this is evident in the strong emphasis in both Finnish documents on support for the AU and other African regional organisations and for regional integration, especially with respect to security and peacekeeping.

Norway

- Norway's Africa strategy has the most special features, partly because Norway is outside the EU, so that the scope for individual initiatives is wider. The strategy includes a number of elements unique among the four countries and reflecting special Norwegian competence and hence business opportunities for Norwegian firms. The trends in *The Platform* are further enhanced in *Climate, Conflict and Capital*.
- The Oil for Development and the Extractive Industries Transparency Initiative projects are, for example, combined with a view to promoting national commercial interests.
- Norway's policy documents do not discuss the importance of concentrating development cooperation on fewer countries or sectors in each country. Instead, there is informal discussion of the need to limit the global initiatives and programmes launched or supported by the Norwegian government in line with existing capacity to manage them.
- Norway is so focused on thematic initiatives and global public goods that the implementation of Norwegian-funded initiatives close to the MDGs, such as health and primary education, is included in budget support programmes or outsourced mainly to multilateral organisations. The argument for this approach is that Norway has no unique competence in these fields, so that so-called "bulk aid" – the transfer of just capital and generally available skills – is appropriate.

- The effect of the growing number of international initiatives supported and sometimes initiated by Norway is that the share of traditional long-term bilateral agreements with African partner countries is diminishing. According to the Norwegian development budget for 2011, the share of the "unspecified global" budget line has doubled from 21 per cent in 2006 to 42 per cent in 2009, while the share of bilateral aid with Africa has been reduced. In this regard, Norway can be regarded as a frontrunner in an ongoing international trend.
- Norway is the only Nordic country to stress the importance of combating illicit capital outflows, which erode government revenues in many African countries. Internationally, Norway has cooperated with the likes of France in this field, while there has been little interest in it in other Nordic countries.
- Norway is the only Nordic country with a special programme to monitor international fishing off the coasts of Africa.
- Norway took the initiative on the Commission on the Limits of the Continental Shelf and is the largest contributor to the UN fund to document the outer limits of continental shelves.
- The Oil for Development Initiative draws on Norway's own experience and competence with oil exploration and handling oil revenues.
- With respect to the Climate and Forest Initiative, in Africa Norway gives highest priority to the Congo Basin, but also to Tanzania.
- Norway supports Zambia in its efforts to renegotiate unfavourable mining contracts.
- Norway is the only Nordic country not to register bilateral debt cancellation as ODA in DAC statistics.

In sum, Norway is the Nordic country that focuses most strongly on contributing to global public goods. Traditional long-term bilateral cooperation has in recent years been put on the back-burner. Put differently, Norway now has the most politicised aid programme among the Nordics.

Sweden

- The Policy for Global Development perspective permeates Swedish Africa policy. One of the strongest features of 2003 government bill on the Policy for Global Development is the focus on policy coherence. Sweden is still in the forefront in this regard (at least in the political rhetoric), although the other Nordic countries are following suit, as are EU countries and the EC, which has played a pioneering role.
- Sweden, like Denmark, has decided to reduce the number of long-term development partner countries, and has adopted exit strategies for 23 of them. The implementation of this decision is taking time and it is not yet very visible in

Swedish aid statistics. The responsible minister has indicated further reductions in the number of long-term cooperation partners.
- A parallel reduction in the number of cooperation sectors in each partner country has been decided upon, with similar challenges for implementation. This decision is highly relevant to Africa, as many of Sweden's development partner countries in sub-Saharan Africa have the most diversified development cooperation portfolios.
- Additional instruments have been introduced for private sector support and old instruments have been replaced. In this regard, Sweden's approach has been similar to Denmark's.
- Although the trend is apparent in all Nordic countries, Sweden most strongly emphasises the need for results-based management and measurable aid results in its policy statements. This has influenced the allocation of Swedish aid but so far limited systematic information on the results is traceable. Swedish policy statements also highlight the "open aid" concept, aimed at providing more transparent information on the results of Swedish aid to a broader public and widening the number of actors engaged in development cooperation. The implementation of the transparency element of the policy is, however, ambiguous, in that it is combined with efforts to reduce the support to CSO:s for information purposes.
- Swedish Africa policy highlights the importance of building African research capacity, a priority not evident in the documents of the other Nordic countries. However, it is one of the initiatives suggested in the report of the Africa Commission.

In short, Sweden is a front runner regarding coherence between policy areas and possibly also in stressing results-based management. It is also apparent that the focus areas and thinking about aid policy of Sweden and Denmark are becoming increasingly similar.

6. Summary and Conclusions

Section 4 showed that the current Africa policy-guiding documents of the Nordic countries have a number of basic features in common, a partial reflection of their historically similar general development cooperation policies. All the documents strongly stress poverty reduction as an overall objective, with the MDGs, economic growth and trade, peace and security, democracy and human rights, gender equality, support for regional integration in Africa and coherence across policy areas as important priorities.

Nordic expansion of trade, FDI and other commercial flows has increased, albeit modestly. Africa is still marginal to Nordic commerce and vice versa. Among the Nordics, Norway shows signs of slightly more dynamic development policies.

Denmark, Norway and Sweden have consistently disbursed aid above the DAC-level of 0.7 per cent of GNI, a level Finland reached in 1990, before rapidly falling to much lower levels in the wake of the financial crisis during the 1990s. However, Finland is presently on its way to achieving the EU commitment of 0.7 per cent by 2015.

The three EU members, Denmark, Finland and Sweden, strongly support the EU's role as an important international actor, and also recognise their ability to strengthen their own influence through EU institutions.

As elaborated in the previous section, there are also a number of differences among the Africa policies and strategies of the Nordic countries, giving them increasingly different profiles. Norway is in the vanguard regarding initiatives and programmes to provide or strengthen global public goods and international governance, at the same time opening up markets for internationally competitive Norwegian companies. Denmark is the strongest actor in facilitating Africa's inclusion in a globalising world and promoting commercial and other relations outside development cooperation with Africa. Sweden leads in the field of improving coherence between policy areas. Finland continues to focus on increased sustainable development and the MDGs within traditional long-term bilateral development relations.

The Nordic countries' development policies are gradually diverging even as some of the traditional features remain, and intense cooperation at the operational level continues. For Denmark, Finland and Sweden, development policy is influenced by their EU membership, which also provides these countries with the opportunity to influence a large part of total aid. At the same time, membership reduces the possibilities for an independent Nordic development cooperation profile. Norway is, by contrast, a free-wheeler.

The Nordic countries' strong emphasis on partnership and efforts to ensure the cooperating partners own the aid-supported projects and programmes have weakened, except in the case of Finland. This is ironic, given strong Nordic support for the Paris Declaration, but it is in line with mainstream DAC policy.

The comparison of Nordic Africa policy-guiding documents gives rise to a number of reflections and conclusions on two issues. The first relates to the role a regional policy document can play and the second relates to current trends in and the future role of Nordic relations with Africa, in particular in the field of development cooperation.

Role of Africa policy/strategy documents

Theoretically a hierarchy of development-cooperation policy documents can be identified, with the general ones at the highest level and Africa policies/strategies at an intermediate level, adjusting general policy to an assumed regional framework and guiding country-specific policies and strategies. In practice, this is only partly true, as the main role of the Africa documents seems to be the codification of existing thinking on development and other issue areas at the specific moment the document is launched.

Another aim of the documents is to signal to the international community and/or the domestic political and public arena that the government is aware of the ongoing changes and intends to address them. A related aim may be to avoid the impression that Africa has been forgotten, should more spectacular development occurs in other parts of the world. An Africa strategy may also reflect general political interest in increasing government engagement in Africa, based on security, climate, commercial and continuing development interests.

Still another aim is to codify existing policies and operations, thereby creating a common knowledge base and perception of African development among stakeholders in each of the Nordic countries. This was stressed by many of the interviewees, who commonly expressed the view that the process of working out the Africa policy/strategy was more important than its implementation. From this perspective, the Africa policy process may be regarded as an internal workshop for various stakeholders in Nordic countries involved in relations with Africa in order to build a general consensus and provide a common general framework.

Operationally, the leverage of the Africa documents is normally weak. Interviewees indicated that these documents are seldom used or referred to in policy dialogues with and operations in individual partner countries, although this situation differs among the four countries. However, it was pointed out that they are used when instructions for individual country strategies are given.

It goes without saying that the Nordic countries' Africa relations are influenced by factors other than policy documents. Changes in the real world sometimes happen so rapidly that policy documents are quickly rendered obsolete. In development cooperation, international trends in development research and in the international aid community are changing, in turn influencing development cooperation policies of the Nordic countries. Denmark, Finland and Sweden, as EU members, are also dependent on EU decisions.

African governments today have access to resources beyond those provided by Western aid agencies, both from emerging markets in the form of aid and financial packages and from a larger segment of the private sector. This situation makes possible a new attitude towards Western governments. Increasingly, African governments, some of them major aid recipients, are less interested in dialogue on issues such as governance, human rights and democracy, traditionally high priorities in Nordic Africa development policy. Significant efforts are necessary to analyse this new framework for Nordic relations with Africa in order to identify new measures and instruments for furthering future Nordic relations with Africa.

Eroded Nordic aid model and the split among the Nordics

With regard to the "joint Nordic aid model", the documents analysed, and still more the developments since they were published, indicate that there is today a very weak basis for using the term. Denmark and Sweden are moving in one direction, Norway in another, while Finland is the sole remaining guardian of what once was the Nordic aid model.[31]

In recent years, Nordic cooperation has been increasingly guided by what happens in major international venues, particularly the EU. The importance of specific Nordic cooperation may erode as the relevant constellations of countries and international organisations vary, depending on the specific programmes in each of the partner countries. However, the existence of other constellations – be it the Nordic+ group, the EU or others under formation – does not preclude Nordic cooperation when common policy positions are being prepared within a wider group. Nonetheless, depending on the issue, constellations may contain fewer Nordic countries and more other players.

As noted in section 2, there is a long tradition of Nordic cooperation in Africa. At least since the mid-1990s, this approach has gradually weakened. Still, the Africa policy-guiding documents reflect some remnant of this cooperative spirit and include occasional statements expressing political will to continue such cooperation. For a long period, the closest cooperation was between Norway and Sweden. More recently, Norway seems to be seeking more transatlantic inspiration, with reduced interest in Nordic cooperation, including with Sweden. This trend is accentuated by Norway's status as a non-member of the EU, which affords it wider scope for individual initiatives and results in the efforts

---

31. *Development Today*, no. 21–22, 2010 contains a number of articles on this theme, based on actual policy development over the past 20 years.

mentioned in section 5 to align the country with donors interested in international initiatives.

Traditionally, Denmark has for many years been seen by the other Nordics as being less enthusiastic about operating at a Nordic level, although at the very beginning Denmark was the main driver of Nordic cooperation, including joint activities. In recent years, however, Sweden and Denmark seem to have moved closer at the political level, and some of their development cooperation reforms seem to have been mutually inspired.

Sweden and Denmark are preparing to form a loose alliance with donors such as Germany, the UK, Canada and USAID with the aim of influencing the future DAC agenda. The focus seems to be on strengthening global public goods in areas such as climate, health security, migration, food security, stabilising fragile states and so on. Another priority is making international aid more results-based, while a third is working increasingly through the private sector to promote economic growth.

In development policy, the Nordic countries thus no longer form the core of a like-minded group. Instead, they are moving along different trajectories and in the process joining new donor constellations.

Despite this development at the policy level, operational-level cooperation among Nordic embassies remains very strong in many African partner countries. This cooperation often arises from donor harmonisation rather than from Nordic countries as a group cooperating with the host country government. The level and form of cooperation shifts with the content of particular national programmes, the personal "chemistry" between personalities stationed at a given time and the attitude of the local EU community.

A recent instrument generating increased cooperation among Nordic embassies all over the world is the Stoltenberg Report from 2009, which includes recommendations on increased cooperation in foreign and particularly security policy. The Nordic Council of Foreign Ministers decided in two meetings during 2010 on such increased cooperation, and interviews confirm such a trend in at least some African countries.

Other arenas for intense Nordic operational cooperation are the meetings and decision-making processes in a large number of multilateral organisations, many of them part of the UN family. The joint Nordic/Baltic executive directorships in the World Bank, IMF and African Development Bank also generate intense Nordic cooperation, including on Africa.

If there is political will – possible areas for improved Nordic cooperation

In spite of the erosion of the "Nordic aid model", several options for increased Nordic cooperation emerge from the Africa documents and the interviews for this study, should the political will for joint or coordinated policy grow within Nordic governments:

- Strengthened influence on the EU's Africa policy, through enhanced common preparations and action among Nordic EU members.
- More joint analytical work, including analytical work and joint efforts by researchers and experts from both the Nordic countries and Africa. NAI is one possible arena for such activities.
- Strengthened Nordic cooperation to improve coordination, planning and information-exchanges in support of African capacity-building.
- Linked to this is restoring Nordic cooperation in support of African research capacity.
- Smarter and more intense links between Nordic field offices and Nordic executive director offices in the World Bank, IMF and AfDB.
- Further improvement of Nordic cooperation and division of labour in local harmonisation processes in numerous partner countries where all or several Nordic countries are represented.
- A more radical option would be for Nordic countries to divide among themselves the long-term cooperating countries in Africa, so that each Nordic country takes responsibility for a few partner countries and vacates the rest. Each Nordic country would then become a major donor in a few countries, as the volume of their aid would be consistent with current joint Nordic aid levels.

References

Policy/strategy documents

DENMARK

Denmark in Africa – A continent on its way. The Government's priorities for Denmark's cooperation with sub-Saharan Africa (August 2007).

Realising the Potential of Africa's Youth. Report of the Africa Commission (May 2009).

Freedom from Poverty, Freedom to Change (May 2010).

FINLAND

Africa in Finland's development politics. Finland's development policy framework programme. (July 2009).

Africa in Finnish Foreign Policy (February 2010).

Development Policy Programme. Towards a Sustainable and Just World Community. Government Decision in Principle (2007).

NORWAY

Platform for an integrated Africa policy. (December 2008).

Climate, Conflict and Change. Norwegian development policy adapting to change. Government Report nr. 13 (2008-09) to the Storting.

SWEDEN

Sweden and Africa – a policy to address common challenges and opportunities (March 2008).

Shared Responsibility. Sweden's Policy for Global Development. Government Bill 2002/03:122.

Global Challenges – Our Responsibility Government Communication 2007/2008:89.

Other literature

Billing, A. and C. Carlsson (2008). *Kibaha Education Centre. A sustainable development cooperation project?* Göteborg: University of Göteborg, School of Global Studies.

Brautigam, D. (2009). *The Dragon's Gift. The real story of China in Africa.* Oxford: Oxford University Press.

Cheru, F. and C. Obi (eds) (2010). *The Role of China and India in Africa. Challenges, Opportunities and Critical Interventions.* London: Zed Books.

Commission on Climate Change and Development (2009). *Closing the Gaps.* Stockholm.

Friis Bach, C. and T. Borring Olesen, S. Kaur-Pedersen and J. Pedersen, (2008). *Idealer og realiteter. Dansk udviklingspolitiks historie 1945-2005*. Köbenhavn: Gyldendal.

Haarlöv, J. (1988). *Regional Cooperation in Southern Africa*. CDR Research Report, no. 14.

Koponen, J. and H. Heinonen (2002). "Africa in Finnish policy – deepening involvement" in Wohlgemuth, L. (ed.). *The Nordic Countries and Africa – Old and New Relations*. Uppsala: The Nordic Africa Institute.

OECD (1985). *Twenty-five years of development cooperation. A review.* Paris. OECD.

OECD Development Centre (2009): *The rise of China and India: What's in it for Africa?*

OECD/DAC (2009). *Peer Review Sweden.* Paris: OECD.

OECD (2010). *Perspectives on Global Development, 2010: Shifting Wealth*. Paris: OECD.

Radelet, S. (2010). *Emerging Africa: How 17 Countries Are Leading the Way*. Washington DC: Center for Global Development.

Selbervik, H. with K. Nygaard (2006). Nordic *Exceptionalism in Development Assitance? Aid Policies and the Major donors: The Nordic countries*. Bergen: CMI Report R 2006:8.

Sogge, D. (2002). *Give and Take, What's the Matter with Foreign Aid?* London: Zed Books.

SOU 1992:124. *Bistånd under omprövning. Översyn av det svenska utvecklingssamarbetet med Moçambique*.

Sellström, T. (2002*). Sweden and National Liberation in Southern Africa. Vol II. Solidarity and Assistance 1970-1994*. Uppsala: TheNordic Africa Institute.

Stoltenberg, T. (2009). *Nordisk samarbeid om utenriks- og Sikkerhetspolitikk.* Forslag overlevert de nordiske utenriksministere på extraordinärt nordiskt utenriksministermöte. Oslo 9 February 2009.

Wohlgemuth, L. (ed.) (2002). *The Nordic Countries and Africa. Old and New Relations*. Uppsala: The Nordic Africa Institute.

Interviews

DENMARK
Lars Engberg-Pedersen, DIIS
Johnny Flentö, MFA
Nanna Hviidt, DIIS
Mette Knudsen, MFA
Sanne Olsen, MFA
Klaus Winkel, consultant

FINLAND
Helena Airaaksinen, MFA
Kari Alanko, MFA
Seppo Kalliokoski, Finnish-Namibian society/KEPA
Kirsti Kauppi, MFA
Juhani Koponen, IDS, University of Helsinki
Nina Näsman, MFA
Jorma Suvanto, MFA
Heikki Tuuanen, MFA

NORWAY
Magnus Björnsen, Norwegian Council for Africa
Kjell Harald Dalen, MFA
Agnete Eriksen, f.d. Norad
Tore Linné-Eriksen, Oslo Högskole
Stein Sundstöl Eriksen, NUPI
Tore Gjöes, MFA
Kjetil Fred Hansen, Oslo Högskole
Hege Hertz, MFA
Robert Hovde, MFA
Mette Masst, MFA
Tore Nedrebö, MFA
Atle Sommerfeld, Kirkens Nödhjelp
Tone Tinnes, MFA

SWEDEN
Georg Andrén, MFA
Marina Berg, MFA
Thomas Brundin, MFA
Per-Eric Högberg, MFA
Anton Johnston, MFA
Kristina Kühnel, Sida
Sten Rylander, MFA
Ingrid Wetterqvist, MFA
Berit Wiklund, Africa Groups of Sweden
Lennart Wohlgemuth, Gothenburg University
Erik Åberg, MFA
Torvald Åkesson, MFA

Table Annex

1. a-c. ODA shares to sub-Saharan Africa from Nordic countries.
2. ODA costs for refugees in donor countries 2005–08.
3. ODA costs for debt relief 2005–08.
4. ODA countries long-term development partners in Africa.
5. 20 largest sub-Saharan African recipient countries 2008.
6. Nordic countries and the Commitment to Development Index 2006–10.
7. Nordic countries and the Commitment to Development Index 2010.
8. Paris Declaration indicators – Nordic countries 2005–07.
9. Paris Declaration indicators – Sweden 2005–09.
10. Nordic countries trade with sub-Saharan Africa, 2005–09.

Tables 1 a–c ODA share to sub-Saharan Africa from Nordic countries

Tables 1 a–b are based on DAC statistics, showing actual disbursements, including ex-post allocated humanitarian assistance and other forms of aid not geographically allocated in the budget. Table 1c, on the other hand, is based on budget figures. Figures are, therefore, not compatible and they show strong differences in levels. They, therefore, mainly show the trend in each Nordic country and for each of the tables compare the relative level of the four countries.

Table 1a. ODA share to sub-Saharan Africa from Nordic countries
(Percentage of total bilateral gross disbursements, excluding amounts unspecified by region)

Year	Denmark	Finland	Norway	Sweden	EC
2000–01	52.2	41.2	41.5	42.5	33.6
2001–02	50.8	42.6	42.2	43.8	38.5
2002–03	50.6	44.7	45.8	50.8	44.0
2003–04	51.9	47.4	47.8	50.9	44.3
2004–05	52.7	35.4	47.2	49.7	43.4
2005–06	56.4	38.3	48.5	47.1	42.2
2006–07	59.0	50.0	48.0	48.8	43.1
2007–08	59.1	50.1	49.0	53.1	40.3

OECD: Development Cooperation Reports 2005-10, table 27.

Table 1b. ODA share to sub-Saharan Africa from Nordic countries
(Percentage of donor's total bilateral ODA net disbursements)

Year	Denmark	Finland	Norway	Sweden
2001	39.3	30.9	29.5	26.2
2002	37.6	29.4	34.8	28.5
2003	41.5	33.2	35.4	34.4
2004	41.7	31.1	35.2	29.7
2005	41.3	22.8	32.0	32.7
2006	48.5	36.5	32.6	29.0
2007	50.1	34.8	29.4	31.6
2008	46.0	32.5	31.1	30.1

OECD: Development Cooperation Reports 2006 and 2010, table 29.

Table 1c. Africa's share of the Nordic's total bilateral aid budget 2009–11

Year	Denmark	Finland	Norway	Sweden
2009	56.2 %	59.3 %	62.0 %	32.9 %
2010	49.5 %	58.6 %	62.1 %	37.9 %
2011	55.1 %	60.9 %	61.3 %	36.6 %

Sources: Annual budget bills.

Table 2. ODA costs for refugees in donor countries 2005–08 (US$ million)

Country	2005	2006	2007	2008
Denmark	70	42	45	49
Finland	17	11	18	26
Norway	68	67	78	141
Sweden	143	164	258	375

Source: OECD/DAC: Development Cooperation Report 2010

Table 3. ODA costs for debt relief 2005–08

Country	2005	2006	2007	2008
Denmark	50	146	123	117
Finland	150	–	–	3
Norway	–	–	–	–
Sweden	53	292	74	–

Source: OECD/DAC: Development Cooperation Report 2010

Table 4. Nordic countries' long-term development partners in Africa

Denmark	Finland	Norway	Sweden
Programme countries	*Long-term cooperation countries*	*Cooperation countries in Africa*	*Long-term cooperation countries*
Benin*	Ethiopia	Angola	Burkina Faso
Burkina Faso	Kenya	Burundi	Ethiopia
Ghana	Mozambique	Ethiopia	Kenya
Kenya	Tanzania	DR Congo	Mali
Mali	Zambia	Liberia	Mozambique
Mozambique	*Countries under reconstruction*	Madagascar	Rwanda
Tanzania	Somalia	Malawi	Tanzania
Uganda	Sudan	Mali	Uganda
Zambia*	*Other countries*	Mozambique	Zambia
	Namibia	Somalia	*Conflict and/or post-conflict countries*
Niger	South Africa	South Africa	Burundi
Fragile states		Sudan	DR Congo
Sudan		Tanzania	Liberia
Zimbabwe		Uganda	Sierra Leone
Countries with major regional influence		Zambia	Somalia
South Africa			Sudan
Nigeria			*Selective cooperation countries*
			Botswana
Ethiopia			Namibia
			South Africa
* to be phased out by 2013			

All four Nordic countries thus have only three African countries in common as long-term development partners: Mozambique, Tanzania and Zambia. Three of them have three common African partners: Ethiopia (Fi, No, Swe), Kenya (Da, Fi, Swe) and Uganda (Da, No, Swe).

If we also include other categories of African countries, all four Nordic countries provide significant aid in the form of humanitarian assistance to conflict-ridden countries such as Somalia and Sudan.

Table 5. 20 largest sub-Saharan African recipient countries in 2008

Denmark	Finland	Norway	Sweden	EC	EU total
1. Tanzania	Tanzania	Tanzania	Tanzania	Ethiopia	Ethiopia
2. Mozamb.	Mozambique	Sudan	Mozambique	Sudan	Mozambique
3. Uganda	Zambia	Mozambique	DRC	Uganda	Tanzania
4. Nigeria	Kenya	Uganda	Kenya	DRC	Sudan
5. Ghana	Ethiopia	Zambia	Sudan	Tanzania	DRC
6. Kenya	South Africa	Malawi	Uganda	South Africa	Uganda
7. Benin	Somalia	Somalia	Zambia	Mozambique	Ghana
8. Burkina F	Sudan	Ethiopia	Ethiopia	Niger	South Africa
9. Sudan	Namibia	DRC	Mali	Mali	Liberia
10. Zambia	DRC	Liberia	Liberia	Chad	Kenya
11. South Afr	Uganda	Burundi	Zimbabwe	Burkina Faso	Burkina Faso
12. Somalia	Chad	Madagascar	Somalia	Côte d'Ivoire	Senegal
13. Zimbabw	CAR	Kenya	Burkina Faso	Madagascar	Botswana
14. Niger	Liberia	Zimbabwe	Malawi	Somalia	Zambia
15. Mali	Angola	South Africa	Rwanda	Senegal	Mali
16. Liberia	Malawi	Angola	South Africa	Malawi	Rep Congo
17. Ethiopia	Sierra Leone	Mali	Chad	Benin	Rwanda
18. DRC	Zimbabwe	Namibia	Burundi	Ghana	Malawi
19. Angola	Rwanda	Eritrea	CAR	Zambia	Somalia
20. Malawi	Nigeria	Nigeria	Equa Guinea	Rwanda	Benin

Sources: EU donor Atlas 2010 and for Norway OECD/ CRS statistics

The table shows that 12 countries are among all four Nordic countries' top 20 sub-Saharan African recipients, and another three are on three top-20 lists. Tanzania and Mozambique have for many decades been at the top. Nine of the 12 countries on all Nordic top 20 lists are also on the EC list.

Table 6. Nordic countries and the Commitment to Development Index 2006–10

Ranking Overall CDI

Country	2006	2007	2008	2009	2010
Denmark	2	2	4	2	2
Finland	7	5	7	9	7
Norway	4	3	2	3	4
Sweden	3	3	2	1	1

Ranking Aid

Country	2006	2007	2008	2009	2010
Denmark	1	1	3	2	2
Finland	10	7	7	5	7
Norway	3	4	4	3	4
Sweden	2	2	1	1	1

Ranking Trade

Country	2006	2007	2008	2009	2010
Denmark	11	11	13	16	17
Finland	6	7	5	5	6
Norway	20	20	21	21	21
Sweden	6	11	8	7	8

Source: www.cgdev.org

Table 7. Nordic countries and the Commitment to Development Index 2010

All development countries

Overall	1) Sweden, 2) Denmark, 4) Norway, 7) Finland.
Aid	1) Sweden, 2) Denmark, 4) Norway, 7) Finland.
Trade	6) Finland, 8) Sweden, 17) Denmark, 21) Norway.
Investment	1) Norway, 9) Sweden, 14) Finland, 17) Denmark.
Migration	2) Sweden, 3) Norway, 9) Denmark, 16) Finland.
Environment	1) Finland, 10) Denmark, 13) Sweden, 17) Norway.
Security	4) Norway, 5) Denmark, 6) Finland, 14) Sweden
Technology	7) Denmark, 8) Finland, 9) Norway, 17) Sweden.

Sub-Saharan Africa

Overall	6) Sweden, 7) Denmark, 8) Norway, 12) Finland.
Aid	2) Denmark, 3) Sweden, 5) Norway, 9) Finland
Trade	4) Finland, 6) Sweden, 16) Denmark, 19) Norway.
Investment	1) Norway, 9) Sweden, 14) Finland, 17) Denmark.
Migration	6) Sweden, 9) Norway, 18) Denmark, 19) Finland
Environment	1) Finland, 2) 11) Denmark, 14) Sweden, 18) Norway
Security	6) Norway, 8) Finland, 10) Denmark, 22) Sweden
Technology	7) Denmark, 8) Finland, 9) Norway, 17) Sweden.

Table 8. Paris Declaration indicators 2005-07 – Nordic countries

PD indicator	Denmark 2005	Denmark 2007	Finland 2005	Finland 2007	Norway 2005	Norway 2007	Sweden 2005	Sweden 2007
3. Govt. budget estimates comprehensive and realistic?	47%	66%	32%	58%	57%	66%	35%	51%
4. How much technical assistance is coordinated with country programmes?	45%	75%	52%	68%	75%	57%	62%	51%
5a. How much aid for governments uses country public finance management systems?	29%	54%	32%	59%	60%	59%	47%	57%
5b. How much aid for governments uses country procurement systems?	44%	68%	48%	70%	68%	75%	48%	57%
6. How many parallel project implementation units to country structures?	69	44	9	4	3	7	36	23
7. Are disbursements on schedule and recorded by government?	50%	50%	34%	43%	55%	96%	48%	55%
8. How much bilateral aid is untied?	84%	96%	98%	93%	99%	100%	100%	100%
9. How much aid is programme-based?	60%	64%	38%	62%	37%	49%	49%	47%
How many donor missions are coordinated?	34%	45%	27%	40%	59%	33%	34%	32%
How much country-analysis is coordinated?	80%	89%	58%	77%	77%	87%	34%	65%

Source: 2008 survey on monitoring the Paris Declaration, Vol. 1 Overview. Appendix B

Table 9. Paris Declaration indicators 2005-09 – Sweden

PD Indicator	2005	2007	2007*	2009*
3.Govt. budget estimates comprehensive and realistic?	35%	51%	61%	74%
4. How much TA is coordinated with country programmes?	62%	51%	51%	80%
5a. How much aid uses country PFM systems?	47%	57%	60%	60%
5.b. How much aid uses country procurement systems?	48%	57%	61%	65%
6. How may PIUs parallel to country structures?	36	23	9	7
7. Are disbursements on schedule and recorded by government?	48%	55%	68%	67%
8. How much bilateral aid is untied?	100%	100%		
9. How much aid is programme-based?	49%	47%	47%	57%
How many donor missions are coordinated?	34%	32%	43%	71%
How much country-analysis is coordinated?	34%	65%	55%	65%

Source for 2005 and 2007: 2008 survey on monitoring the Paris Declaration, Vol. 1 Overview. Appendix B

Source for 2007 and 2009: Sidas årsredovisning 2009. Dessa uppgifter är inte jämförbara med de tidigare eftersom de gäller endast de långsiktiga samarbetsländerna.

Table 10. Nordic countries' trade with sub-Saharan Africa 2005–09

Country (currency)	2005	2006	2007	2008	2009
Norway (NOK bn)					
Exports to SSA	3.3	3.3	5.2	5.9	4.9
Exports global	668.8	782.9	795.6	959.0	786.8
SSA as % of global	0.4 %	0.4 %	0.7 %	0.6 %	0.6 %
Imports from SSA	3.9	4.5	5.9	7.9	6.5
Imports global	265.2	304.3	345.0	361.6	307.1
SSA as % of global	1.5 %	1.5 %	1.7 %	2.2 %	2.1 %
Finland (€ mn)					
Exports to SSA	751	941	1050	879	614
Exports global	52,453	61,489	65,688	65,580	44,897
SSA as % of global	1.4	1.5	1.6	1.3	1.4 %
Imports from SSA	215	259	307	449	211
Imports global	47,027	55,253	59,616	62,402	43,250
SSA as % of global	0.5	0.5	0.5	0.7	0.5 %
Denmark (DAK bn)					
Exports to SSA	4.7	5.5	5.7	7.2	5.8
Exports global	501.6	543.8	554.8	550.7	462.0
SSA as % of global	0.9 %	1.0 %	1.0 %	1.3 %	1.3 %
Imports from SSA	2.1	2.3	2.3	2.8	1.8
Imports global	445.8	506.5	538.3	532.4	423.6
SSA as % of global	0.5 %	0.5 %	0.4 %	0.5 %	0.4 %
Sweden (SEK bn)					
Exports to SSA	12.3	12.7	16.0	21.3	18.6
Exports global	970.8	1,089.1	1,140.7	1,194.4	997.9
SSA as % of global	1.3 %	1.2 %	1.4 %	1.8 %	1.9 %
Imports from SSA	3.1	3.4	4.4	7.0	8.5
Imports global	832.6	939.7	1020.3	1097.9	910.9
SSA as % of global	0.4 %	0.4 %	0.4 %	0.6 %	0.9 %

Source: National trade statistics

DISCUSSION PAPERS PUBLISHED BY THE INSTITUTE

Recent issues in the series are available electronically for download free of charge
www.nai.uu.se

1. Kenneth Hermele and Bertil Odén, *Sanctions and Dilemmas. Some Implications of Economic Sanctions against South Africa.*
   1988. 43 pp. ISBN 91-7106-286-6

2. Elling Njål Tjønneland, *Pax Pretoriana. The Fall of Apartheid and the Politics of Regional Destabilisation.*
   1989. 31 pp. ISBN 91-7106-292-0

3. Hans Gustafsson, Bertil Odén and Andreas Tegen, *South African Minerals. An Analysis of Western Dependence.*
   1990. 47 pp. ISBN 91-7106-307-2

4. Bertil Egerö, *South African Bantustans. From Dumping Grounds to Battlefronts.*
   1991. 46 pp. ISBN 91-7106-315-3

5. Carlos Lopes, *Enough is Enough! For an Alternative Diagnosis of the African Crisis.*
   1994. 38 pp. ISBN 91-7106-347-1

6. Annika Dahlberg, *Contesting Views and Changing Paradigms.*
   1994. 59 pp. ISBN 91-7106-357-9

7. Bertil Odén, *Southern African Futures. Critical Factors for Regional Development in Southern Africa.*
   1996. 35 pp. ISBN 91-7106-392-7

8. Colin Leys and Mahmood Mamdani, *Crisis and Reconstruction – African Perspectives.*
   1997. 26 pp. ISBN 91-7106-417-6

9. Gudrun Dahl, *Responsibility and Partnership in Swedish Aid Discourse.*
   2001. 30 pp. ISBN 91-7106-473-7

10. Henning Melber and Christopher Saunders, *Transition in Southern Africa – Comparative Aspects.*
    2001. 28 pp. ISBN 91-7106-480-X

11. *Regionalism and Regional Integration in Africa.*
    2001. 74 pp. ISBN 91-7106-484-2

12. Souleymane Bachir Diagne, et al., *Identity and Beyond: Rethinking Africanity.*
    2001. 33 pp. ISBN 91-7106-487-7

13. Georges Nzongola-Ntalaja, et al., *Africa in the New Millennium.* Edited by Raymond Suttner.
    2001. 53 pp. ISBN 91-7106-488-5

14. *Zimbabwe's Presidential Elections 2002.* Edited by Henning Melber.
    2002. 88 pp. ISBN 91-7106-490-7

15. Birgit Brock-Utne, *Language, Education and Democracy in Africa.*
    2002. 47 pp. ISBN 91-7106-491-5

16. Henning Melber et al., *The New Partnership for Africa's development (NEPAD).*
    2002. 36 pp. ISBN 91-7106-492-3

17. Juma Okuku, *Ethnicity, State Power and the Democratisation Process in Uganda.*
    2002. 42 pp. ISBN 91-7106-493-1

18. Yul Derek Davids, et al., *Measuring Democracy and Human Rights in Southern Africa.* Compiled by Henning Melber.
    2002. 50 pp. ISBN 91-7106-497-4

19. Michael Neocosmos, Raymond Suttner and Ian Taylor, *Political Cultures in Democratic South Africa.* Compiled by Henning Melber.
    2002. 52 pp. ISBN 91-7106-498-2

20. Martin Legassick, *Armed Struggle and Democracy. The Case of South Africa.*
    2002. 53 pp. ISBN 91-7106-504-0

21. Reinhart Kössler, Henning Melber and Per Strand, *Development from Below. A Namibian Case Study.*
    2003. 32 pp. ISBN 91-7106-507-5

22. Fred Hendricks, *Fault-Lines in South African Democracy. Continuing Crises of Inequality and Injustice.*
    2003. 32 pp. ISBN 91-7106-508-3

23. Kenneth Good, *Bushmen and Diamonds. (Un) Civil Society in Botswana.*
    2003. 39 pp. ISBN 91-7106-520-2

24. Robert Kappel, Andreas Mehler, Henning Melber and Anders Danielson, *Structural Stability in an African Context.*
    2003. 55 pp. ISBN 91-7106-521-0

25. Patrick Bond, *South Africa and Global Apartheid. Continental and International Policies and Politics.*
    2004. 45 pp. ISBN 91-7106-523-7

26. Bonnie Campbell (ed.), *Regulating Mining in Africa. For whose benefit?*
    2004. 89 pp. ISBN 91-7106-527-X

27. Suzanne Dansereau and Mario Zamponi, *Zimbabwe – The Political Economy of Decline.* Compiled by Henning Melber.
    2005. 43 pp. ISBN 91-7106-541-5

28. Lars Buur and Helene Maria Kyed, *State Recogni-tion of Traditional Authority in Mozambique. The nexus of Community Representation and State Assist-ance.*
2005. 30 pp. ISBN 91-7106-547-4

29. Hans Eriksson and Björn Hagströmer, *Chad – Towards Democratisation or Petro-Dictatorship?*
2005. 82 pp. ISBN 91-7106-549-

30. Mai Palmberg and Ranka Primorac (eds), *Skinning the Skunk – Facing Zimbabwean Futures.*
2005. 40 pp. ISBN 91-7106-552-0

31. Michael Brüntrup, Henning Melber and Ian Taylor, *Africa, Regional Cooperation and the World Market – Socio-Economic Strategies in Times of Global Trade Regimes.* Com-piled by Henning Melber.
2006. 70 pp. ISBN 91-7106-559-8

32. Fibian Kavulani Lukalo, *Extended Handshake or Wrestling Match? – Youth and Urban Culture Celebrating Politics in Kenya.*
2006. 58 pp. ISBN 91-7106-567-9

33. Tekeste Negash, *Education in Ethiopia: From Crisis to the Brink of Collapse.*
2006. 55 pp. ISBN 91-7106-576-8

34. Fredrik Söderbaum and Ian Taylor (eds) *Micro-Regionalism in West Africa. Evidence from Two Case Studies.*
2006. 32 pp. ISBN 91-7106-584-9

35. Henning Melber (ed.), *On Africa – Scholars and African Studies.*
2006. 68 pp. ISBN 978-91-7106-585-8

36. Amadu Sesay, *Does One Size Fit All? The Sierra Leone Truth and Reconciliation Commission Revisited.*
2007. 56 pp. ISBN 978-91-7106-586-5

37. Karolina Hulterström, Amin Y. Kamete and Henning Melber, *Political Opposition in African Countries – The Case of Kenya, Namibia, Zambia and Zimbabwe.*
2007. 86 pp. ISBN 978-7106-587-2

38. Henning Melber (ed.), *Governance and State Delivery in Southern Africa. Examples from Botswana, Namibia and Zimbabwe.*
2007. 65 pp. ISBN 978-91-7106-587-2

39. Cyril Obi (ed.), *Perspectives on Côte d'Ivoire: Between Political Breakdown and Post-Conflict Peace.*
2007. 66 pp. ISBN 978-91-7106-606-6

40. Anna Chitando, *Imagining a Peaceful Society. A Vision of Children's Literature in a Post-Conflict Zimbabwe.*
2008. 26 pp. ISBN 978-91-7106-623-7

41. Olawale Ismail, *The Dynamics of Post-Conflict Reconstruction and Peace Building in West Africa. Between Change and Stability.*
2009. 52 pp. ISBN 978-91-7106-637-4

42. Ron Sandrey and Hannah Edinger, *Examining the South Africa–China Agricultural Relationship.*
2009. 58 pp. ISBN 978-91-7106-643-5

43. Xuan Gao, *The Proliferation of Anti-Dumping and Poor Governance in Emerging Economies.*
2009. 41 pp. ISBN 978-91-7106-644-2

44. Lawal Mohammed Marafa, *Africa's Business and Development Relationship with China. Seeking Moral and Capital Values of the Last Economic Frontier.*
2009. xx pp. ISBN 978-91-7106-645-9

45. Mwangi wa Githinji, *Is That a Dragon or an Elephant on Your Ladder? The Potential Impact of China and India on Export Led Growth in African Countries.*
2009. 40 pp. ISBN 978-91-7106-646-6

46. Jo-Ansie van Wyk, *Cadres, Capitalists, Elites and Coalitions. The ANC, Business and Development in South Africa.*
2009. 61 pp. ISBN 978-91-7106-656-5

47. Elias Courson, *Movement for the Emancipation of the Niger Delta (MEND). Political Marginalization, Repression and Petro-Insurgency in the Niger Delta.* 2009. 30 pp. ISBN 978-91-7106-657-2

48. Babatunde Ahonsi, *Gender Violence and HIV/AIDS in Post-Conflict West Africa. Issues and Responses.* 2010.
38 pp. ISBN 978-91-7106-665-7

49. Usman Tar and Abba Gana Shettima, *Endangered Democracy? The Struggle over Secularism and its Implications for Politics and Democracy in Nigeria.*
2010. 21 pp. ISBN 978-91-7106-666-4

50. Garth Andrew Myers, *Seven Themes in African Urban Dynamics.* 2010. 28 pp.
ISBN 978-91-7106-677-0

51. Abdoumaliq Simone, *The Social Infrastructures of City Life in Contemporary Africa.*
2010. 33 pp. ISBN 978-91-7106-678-7

52. Li Anshan, *Chinese Medical Cooperation in Africa. With Special Emphasis on the Medical Teams and Anti-Malaria Campaign.*
2011. 24 pp. ISBN 978-91-7106-683-1

53. Folashade Hunsu, *Zangbeto: Navigating the Spaces Between Oral art, Communal Security And Conflict Mediation in Badagry, Nigeria.*
2011. 27 pp. ISBN 978-91-7106-688-6

54. Jeremiah O. Arowosegbe, *Reflections on the Challenge of Reconstructing Post-Conflict States in West Africa: Insights from Claude Ake's Political Writings.*
2011. 40 pp. ISBN 978-91-7106-689-3

55. Bertil Odén, *The Africa Policies of Nordic Countries and the Erosion of the Nordic Aid Model: A comparative study.*
2011. 66 pp. ISBN 978-91-7106-691-6

www.ingramcontent.com/pod-product-compliance
Ingram Content Group UK Ltd.
Pitfield, Milton Keynes, MK11 3LW, UK
UKHW051652180426
11947UKWH00021B/1914